Rothstein, Eric.

PR
698   Restoration trag-
.T7   edy
R68
1978

DATE DUE

JUN 2 1 1999		

Restoration Tragedy

FORM AND THE PROCESS OF CHANGE

Restoration Tragedy

FORM AND THE PROCESS OF CHANGE

BY ERIC ROTHSTEIN

GREENWOOD PRESS, PUBLISHERS
WESTPORT, CONNECTICUT

Library of Congress Cataloging in Publication Data

Rothstein, Eric.
    Restoration tragedy.

    Reprint of the ed. published by the University of
Wisconsin Press, Madison.
    Includes bibliographical references and index.
    1. English drama--Restoration, 1660-1700--History
and criticism. 2. English drama (Tragedy)--History
and criticism. I. Title.
[PR698.T7R68 1978]   822'.051   78-5529
ISBN 0-313-20472-1

Reprinted in 1978 by Greenwood Press, Inc.,
51 Riverside Avenue, Westport, CT. 06880

Printed in the United States of America

10 9 8 7 6 5 4 3 2 1

FOR MY PARENTS
WITHOUT WHOM THIS BOOK WOULD HAVE HAD
NO AUTHOR, THIS AUTHOR NO BOOK

PREFACE

"MUCH NEGLECTED" MAKES AN UNAPPETIZING HORS D'OEUVRE TO a book: most literature that is much neglected ought to be. The neglect of Restoration tragedy, however, seems to me indefensible, explicable only because serious study of the Restoration is comparatively recent. No one who has read sympathetically *All for Love* or *Don Sebastian, The Mourning Bride,* either of Otway's two finest tragedies, or any one of a number of minor but intelligent and skillful tragedies written during the Restoration, will require further apology for the dramatic tradition from which they sprang. He will require, I hope, analysis. As yet that analysis has not been forthcoming, save for articles on individual plays such as *All for Love* and *Venice Preserv'd,* and for the tangential insights provided by useful compendia like the great *London Stage* or Sarup Singh's *The Theory of Drama in the Restoration Period,* by studies of the heroic play, of which the most incisive is Arthur C. Kirsch's *Dryden's Heroic Drama,* and by various discussions of Restoration comedy. Otherwise, little has been done since the pioneer efforts of Summers, Dobrée, and Nicoll.

This book, as its title indicates, attempts to analyze the tragedy of the Restoration, incidentally in terms of individual plays, specifically in terms of the developing genre. By and large, I have tried to avoid detailed criticism of the plays, and have concerned myself only obliquely with literary values. Needless to say, I should hope that a book such as this has direct relevance to, and is even presupposed by, intelligent value judgments and literary discussion. Needless to say, too, I realize that the literary student must "be a critic in order to be an historian . . . unless we want to reduce literary study to a mere listing of books, to annals or a

vii

chronicle."[1] Annals and chronicles of Restoration tragedy are already available, and I have no wish to duplicate them. Admitting my selectivity, then, I have tried to reveal not an array but a pattern. Individual plays appear as examples to reveal this pattern, this web of procedures that constitute, for the Restoration as for any small "age," its conventions.

Besides illuminating Restoration tragedies, and to some extent other Restoration literature, the process that I shall describe is of importance for at least two reasons. First, the adoption of a pathetic drama in the late sixteen hundreds conditioned the entire subsequent development of English tragedy. The demands of an Arthur Miller for passion, empathy, and democracy of feelings are an echo sounding over two and a half centuries. Secondly, the kinds of changes that we find in the fare of the public theatres turn out to be tellingly analogous to the kinds of changes that developed during the eighteenth century in less popular genres, including almost all verse and prose of literary pretensions. Such a priority of the drama is both logical and unique in "neo-classical" criticism. The central problems of eighteenth-century literary theory arise largely from a specific and novel emphasis on the psychology of aesthetic response, and the re-evaluation of traditional attitudes in terms of that emphasis.[2] Of all genres, the drama is by its nature most immediately sensitive to changes in response, since its offerings are constantly (and financially) tested by audiences: there must be uninterrupted mass appeal. Thus public rhetoric is the drama's domain, and plays register changes in the public temper more quickly, more openly, than do comparatively recondite and private forms,

1. René Wellek, "Literary Theory, Criticism, and History," included in *Concepts of Criticism,* ed. Stephen G. Nichols, Jr. (New Haven, 1963), p. 15.

2. As opposed, say, to Romantic criticism, which proceeds from the psychology of aesthetic composition. See R. S. Crane, "English Criticism: Neo-Classical Criticism," in *Dictionary of World Literature,* ed. Joseph T. Shipley (New York, 1953), and the first chapter of Meyer H. Abrams' *The Mirror and the Lamp* (Oxford, 1953).

like poems. Furthermore, the psychology of communication must
be an urgent concern of empirical dramatic critics; since much
late seventeenth-century dramatic criticism, including Dryden's,
was ad hoc, the critics' anticipation of their successors' focal
interests seems quite logical. The study of Restoration tragedy,
by historical accident, becomes a laboratory of sorts for the study
of movement and variation in the eighteenth-century novel and
poem.

With these historical interests in mind, I have tried to proceed
empirically, even nominalistically, in treating the genre "tragedy." That is, I have grouped and described a very large number of those plays labeled "tragedy" on their title pages, and of
plays quite similar in form and tone to those that are labeled
"tragedy." I stress this method of selection and procedure because
"tragedy," now that most developed generic criticism has been
relegated to texts and manifestoes, remains a sole melodious mermaid, all lure and voluptuousness above, all scales and destruction below. This genre seems to tempt the passionate critic into
abstract generalization, as "epic" and "ode" and even "comedy"
do not. One recent book, for example, informs us that "the tragic
personage is broken by forces which can neither be fully understood nor overcome by rational prudence."[3] Such apodictic mys-
tique makes nonsense of *The Conquest of Granada* or *Venice
Preserv'd*; as a matter of fact, the kind of psychological and
mimetic fullness that such a theory supposes also makes nonsense of *Macbeth* and *Antony and Cleopatra,* unless Shakespeare is read through the prisms of *Moby-Dick.*

It is not surprising that the "high priori road" should be both
narrow and crooked—to how many of the extant Greek tragedies
do the theories of Aristotle himself apply?—or that, because its
assumptions are private, it should almost invariably lead to no
fruit. Statements like, "X does (or does not) conform to the rules
laid down in *The Poetics*," or "X should (or should not) produce
in an intelligent trained viewer a reaction similar to that pro-

3. George Steiner, *The Death of Tragedy* (New York, 1961), p. 8.

duced by *King Lear,"* or "X illustrates (or does not) the same view of life as does *Oedipus"* have, at least, a certain potential precision; the statement *"Mourning Becomes Electra* is not a tragedy" merely serves to cast obloquy. To imply that "tragedy" is a universal standard that playwrights should be trying to meet, or are trying to meet and failing, sets up an illusory norm for panegyric or reproach as a clear statement can not do. And the extraordinary variety of the plays in the tradition of Western tragedy emphasizes the privacy and vagueness of that supposed norm. Ludwig Wittgenstein, who wrote that "philosophy, as we use the word, is a fight against the fascination which forms of expression exert upon us," has a passage in his "Blue Book" which is germane:

> [Our] . . . craving for generality is the resultant of a number of tendencies connected with particular philosophical confusions. There is—
>
> (a) The tendency to look for something in common to all the entities which we commonly subsume under a general term . . .
>
> (b) There is a tendency rooted in our usual forms of expression, to think that the man who has learnt to understand a general term, say, the term "leaf," has thereby come to possess a kind of general picture of a leaf, as opposed to pictures of particular leaves . . .
>
> The idea that in order to get clear about the meaning of a general term one had to find the common element in all its applications, has shackled philosophical investigation; for it has not only led to no result, but also made the philosopher dismiss as irrelevant the concrete cases, which alone could have helped him to understand the usage of the general term.[4]

Those critics who choose to "dismiss as irrelevant the concrete cases," who prefer to emulate Lewis Carroll's Humpty Dumpty

4. Ludwig Wittgenstein, *Preliminary Studies for the "Philosophical Investigations" Generally Known as "The Blue and Brown Books"* (New York, 1958), p. 27, pp. 17–20.

(that lofty autolexicographer), are of course free to do so; but they should remember Alice's parting observation, "Of all the unsatisfactory—," as well as Humpty Dumpty's developing— alas—a tragic flaw.

I have tried to evade such a fate by treating tragedy not as a Being—luminous, normative, enticing, and inaccessible; but as a mere verbal tool with the function of parenthesizing and order- ing certain plays and groups of plays that are demonstrably interrelated. These relations, in turn, must be defined in terms of specific temporal and intellectual contexts, of techniques and goals, of immediate concrete pressures. And here "tragedy," not our term but Dryden's and Settle's and Rowe's, becomes useful as a controlling critical idea in playwrights' and audiences' minds.

With some misgivings I have left out of consideration the Restoration plays translated from French or Italian, Latin or Greek or Spanish; I have also left out adaptations of earlier English plays, such as the various reworkings of Shakespeare, Mrs. Behn's *Abdelazar* (from *Lust's Dominion*), and even Rob- ert Howard's *The Duke of Lerma*. The problems created by these amalgamated texts would have required an extraordinary, and a disproportionate, amount of space.

For those few Restoration tragedians who have been well edited—Otway, Lee, and Boyle in their entirety, and a very small number of plays by others—I have used the modern edi- tions. Because these editions include stop-press variants as well as later auctorial revisions, they are more reliable textually than any actual early edition of the play in question. Furthermore, they are more readily available for reference than are the original texts. In the vast majority of cases, however, the original texts are the only ones available at all that make any claim to accuracy, and for these plays I have in every instance used a copy of the first edition. Thus, unless there is a note specifying the source of a quotation from a play, it should be assumed that the page or signature reference is to the first edition. Transcriptions follow the copy text, except in disregarding typographical conventions in the use of *i* and *j*, *u* and *v*, *vv* (for *w*), and in the italicization of prologues, epilogues, and songs. All translations are mine unless I have indicated otherwise.

A slightly different form of Chapter 1 first appeared in my article, "English Tragic Theory in the Late Seventeenth Century," in *ELH, A Journal of English Literary History,* XXIX (1962). I wish to thank the editors for their courteous permission to reprint this material. I wish to thank, too, the staffs of the Rare Book Room in the Firestone Library at Princeton University, of the Memorial Library at the University of Wisconsin, and of the North Library of the British Museum for their considerate help. Miss Patricia Boyce has typed two versions of this manuscript fast and accurately.

I owe an inestimable debt to Professors Alan S. Downer and G. E. Bentley as teachers and advisors as well as critics of this book. Professor Arthur C. Kirsch has been generous with both suggestions and encouragement, as has my senior colleague, Professor Ricardo B. Quintana. Professor Frank Kearful toiled scrupulously and lucidly through a large portion of the manuscript, from which he helped clean away *bêtises*. My wife has sustained me in mind and spirit through all the weariness, the bemusement, and the putting up with petty crises that the writing of this book has brought. To all these, mere thanks is meager acknowledgment.

E. R.

Madison, Wisconsin
December, 1966

CONTENTS

I

CRITICAL MANEUVERS

TRAGIC THEORY IN THE
RESTORATION

RESTORATION TRAGIC THEORY DEVELOPED, LIKE RESTORATION
tragedy, by subverting the tradition on which it drew. By a sort of
half-aware fifth column work, camouflaged with cheerfully
ambiguous terminology, it so reviewed and revised and remolded
its Renaissance critical models that by the end of the century it
had put in power a new and extraordinarily stable set of doctrines.
Thus adequate rationale was provided for the emotional, "sentimental" tragedy of the post-heroic years. No one cared to question,
or had to question, the commonplace that tragedy should have, in
some way, a didactic moral purpose. But that final cause, which so
dominated medieval and Renaissance criticism,[1] lost its determin-
ing force as Restoration empiricists interested themselves more
and more in efficient causes, in finding out how tragedy worked.

There are two broad explanations of the moral effect of tragedy: they may be called the "fabulist" and the "affective." The
fabulist explanation is the basis for the medieval and Renaissance apology for poetry. It originates in the implied disjunction
of Horace's *utile* and *dulce* (or *prodesse* and *delectare*) and
supposes that one can separate a literary work into a moral fable
on the one hand and "sweet" embellishments on the other. As
the Horatian balance between the two is tilted in favor of the
moral, the embellishments begin to function as persuasives, en-

1. For a general statement of Renaissance didacticism, see Madeleine
Doran, *Endeavors of Art: A Study of Form in the Elizabethan Drama*
(Madison, 1954). For Continental theory in accord with the British, see
Warner Forrest Patterson, *Three Centuries of French Poetic Theory* . . .
(1328–1630), 2 vols. (Ann Arbor, 1935); Bernard Weinberg, *A History of
Literary Criticism in the Italian Renaissance*, 2 vols. (Chicago, 1961); René
Bray, *La formation de la doctrine classique en France* (Paris, 1927).

ticing the reader or spectator through the disguised precepts of virtue so that he may not only learn them but keep pleasant recollections of having done so. In other words, art, *qua* art, is to act as rhetoric. This conception of literary function is a familiar one: it comes up in the classics with, for instance, Lucretius (*De Rerum Natura* IV.10–25); in the Middle Ages with St. Augustine or Boccaccio's *De Genealogia Deorum;* and in the English Renaissance with Harington's description of a "good and honest and wholesome Allegorie . . . hidden in a pleasaunt, and pretie fiction," or his praise of verse for its "pleasure and sweetnesse to the eare which makes the discourse pleasaunt unto us often time when the matter it selfe is harsh and unacceptable."[2]

The affective explanation derives from Aristotle. It holds that the emotions aroused by tragedy, usually some specific emotions, themselves act as the agents of moral force. Unlike fabulist theories, which almost always are general postulations about the nature of art, thus forcing the particular application to tragedy to be made deductively (or, as it turns out, a fortiori), affective theories imply a fully discriminated generic criticism. The earliest English affective theory appears, inchoate, in Sidney's discussion of tragedy. Sidney speaks in *The Apologie* of the merits of the tragic fable, saying that it "openeth the greatest wounds, and sheweth forth the Ulcers that are covered with Tissue; that maketh Kinges fear to be Tyrants . . ." However, he deviates from his English contemporaries by attributing these lessons of mutability to the tragedy's "sturring the affects of admiration and commiseration," even though he does not explain how these affects work. And finally, to show how much tragedy "can moove," he tells the story of an "abhominable Tyrant" who wept at the "sweet violence" on stage despite his having done, remorselessly, far more brutal things himself. Sidney concludes that if the tragedy did the tyrant no good, it was because he

2. *Elizabethan Critical Essays*, ed. G. Gregory Smith, 2 vols. (Oxford, 1904), II, 206.

"withdrewe himselfe from harkening to that which might molli-
fie his hardened heart."[3] Like later theorists, Sidney heavily
stresses a specific tragic emotional reaction rather than the less
differentiated *delectatio* of the Horatian maxim and of most
Renaissance fabulist theory. If one is justified in emphasizing
and extrapolating from "sturring the affects of admiration and
commiseration," Sidney is here providing both a general statement and an empirical example of tragedy's working through
that specific reaction.

Sidney's compatriots were fabulists; his genuflection to affective principles was unique in England, where critics seem to
have paid little attention to even the vaguest Aristotelianism, the
most thoroughly redacted versions of *The Poetics*, until the early
1670's. Curiously enough, the critic who is now scorned as the
most stringently Aristotelian, the translator responsible for bringing out the first English version of any commentary (Rapin's) on
Aristotle's *Poetics*, provides in his own criticism the best and
most conservative exposition of fabulist theory in the Restoration. I am speaking, of course, of Thomas Rymer. Rymer's
conception of the decorum of plot is social rather than aesthetic;
that is, he concerns himself with plot as ideal didactic pattern.
For example, his objection to a man's being killed by a woman in
a play, although he alleges "poetical decency" as the basis of it,
arises not from the rules of the tragic genre, but from a literal
application of the plot to real life at every point, in this case, to
life considered as an ideal social structure. (Such objections
differ in kind from, say, Rymer's objection to blank verse as a
medium proper for the epic.) Besides making these immediate
applications along the way, Rymer analyzes what he calls the
"fable" of each play, expounding it in terms of a presupposed
moral lesson. For the working of that lesson through the fable,
Rymer coined the term "poetical justice." Poetic(al) justice is
the dramatic analogue to Divine Providence, and in Rymer's

3. *Elizabethan Critical Essays*, I, 177–178.

criticism it is equally all-pervasive. His own heroic play, *Edgar* (1678), practices the exact allotment of rewards and punishments upon which his principles insist; and his suggested rewritings of other people's plays further demonstrate the specific application of his strict fabulist doctrines. For instance, he suggests that *Othello* might better have ended with Desdemona alive, for as the play is, it falsifies the moral structure of Providence and the teachings of prudential morality: ". . . we [may] ask here what unnatural crime *Desdemona* or her Parents had committed, to bring this Judgment down upon her; to Wed a Black-amoor, and innocent to be thus cruelly murder'd by him. What instruction can we make out of this Catastrophe? Or whither must our reflection lead us? Is not this to envenome and sour our spirits, to make us repine and grumble at Providence; and the government of the World? If this be our end, what boots it to be Vertuous?"[4]

Although Rymer says that in tragedy "[n]ought [is] intended but pitty and terror," he seems to take the area defined by the causes of those two responses as the area assigned to tragedy by poetic decorum rather than as the distinctive source of the tragic effect. He carries through the Horatian disjunction between *utile* and *dulce* even while entwining them: "I am confident whoever writes a Tragedy cannot please but must also profit; 'tis the Physick of the mind that he makes palatable." Catharsis is skimmed past for the delights of observing the beauty of God's dispensation: "And besides the *purging* of the *passions;* something must stick by observing that constant order, that harmony and beauty of Providence, that necessary relation and chain, whereby the causes and the effects, the vertues and rewards, the vices and their punishments are proportion'd and link'd together; how deep and dark soever are laid the Springs, and however intricate and involv'd are their operations."[5]

4. "A Short View of Tragedy," in *The Critical Works of Thomas Rymer,* ed. Curt A. Zimansky (New Haven, 1956), p. 161.
5. "Tragedies of the Last Age," *Critical Works,* pp. 67, 75, 75.

Rymer's criticism represents the fabulist tradition at its least yielding. Yet during the course of the late seventeenth century that tradition permitted the enemy, popular and chaotic sentiment, to ambush from within. The *delectare* of the Horatian synthesis provided the crevice through which sentimentality was to infiltrate. Moving the passions had always been a function of tragic rhetoric, of tragedy as rhetoric. In the seventeenth century, the suppositions as to the source of rhetorical effectiveness changed, and the necessity for maintaining the traditional kind of emotional response seemed to prescribe abandoning the traditional rhetorical methods. Within the confines of fabulist theory, entirely apart from Aristotelianism, a new kind of dramaturgy was not only authorized but demanded.

Two popular theories were used, up to the middle of the seventeenth century, to account for the nature of tragic pleasure.[6] One is an aesthetic theory, attributing the spectator's delight to the poet's skill. Intrigue, the "underwalks" and interweavings, peripatetic revelations properly set forth in harmonious numbers: these were the reasons for playgoers' relishing theatrical distress. The second theory is the one Rymer advances, that the triumph of virtue and the workings of Providence provide tragic delight. The two theories together form a comprehensive, although limited, way of dealing with dramatic pleasure. If a play is taken, however loosely, as the mediator between expression and action, Providence would be the connection between the play and the action (since, considered in total didactic context, all action must be providential), and poetic skill the connection between the play and artistic expression. Through one the play partakes of nature; through the other, of art. As with fabulist explanations of the function of tragedy, neither the providential nor the aesthetic explanation has generic limitations: both apply equally to all art. Furthermore, neither specifically invites emotionalism; quite on the contrary, both

6. Earl Wasserman, "The Pleasures of Tragedy," *ELH, A Journal of English Literary History,* XIV (1947), 283–307.

presuppose that aloofness which would permit Providence and craftsmanship to be appreciated. Each requires the spectator to have a view of the play as a whole, for Providence and craftsmanship alike can only be enjoyed to the full when the play is over: the experience of pleasure is a recollection of order in the reflecting play as in the reflected world, in the poet's dispensation and God's. That sense of order and propriety is what elevated decorum to its high position.

About the middle of the seventeenth century, a new pair of theories supplanted the old in popularity. One, proceeding from Descartes' physiology, held that the excitation of the passions was itself a sort of inner sensuality; the other, proceeding from Hobbes' psychology, that the feeling of personal satisfaction at their own relative safety shielded the witnesses of theatrical distress from the otherwise unmixed pain of their bared emotions.[7] Quite obviously, these new theories differ radically from the old. Both of them work from the emotional situation rather than from the total order of the play: they call for drama with more passion, more distress; in short, for drama concentrated in a succession of moments, a series of effective incidents rather than a ramified totality. (One might make tentative analogies between these new concepts and the atomism involved in both Hobbesian and Cartesian principles of extension and motion, an atomism which was at about this time reaching the analytic extreme of Leibniz' monadology.) By implication, decorum and craftsmanship are forced to cede to the skillful arrangement of moving circumstances. The rhetorical basis of tragedy had changed. To be persuasive, pleasure had to be deeply satisfying; to be satisfying, it demanded sensationalism; and sensationalism, in turn, bludgeoned the sense of a providential whole out of recognition. For although logically the fabulist theory was ten-

7. Wasserman's discussion of this Hobbesian theory should be read in conjunction with that of Baxter Hathaway, "The Lucretian Return upon Ourselves in Eighteenth-Century Theories of Tragedy," *PMLA*, LXII (1947), 672–689.

able even after the older assumptions about tragic pleasure had
shrunk in prominence, playgoers accustomed to looking for a
succession of sensations rather than for overall order must have
found it difficult to perceive a continuing and exact Providence
animating the whole. Playwrights tried open labeling of their
moral contrivances through maxims and reflections. However,
such reconciliations of *utile* and *dulce* were at best uneasy.
Englishmen wanted to justify, critically, an emotional serial
drama, not only because it was more immediately entertaining
but also because its larval form, the tragicomedies of Fletcher
and the late heroic play, was at the time dominant on the stage.
This desire for critical justification, for exalting the individual
emotional moment in theory as it was being exalted in practice,
drove Restoration critics toward the new (scientific) theories of
tragic pleasure discussed above. It also drove them toward a
non-rhetorical, affective, theory of tragedy.

The source of affective theories, Aristotle's *Poetics,* was not a
popular book in seventeenth-century England. The *Short-Title
Catalogues* of Pollard and Redgrave, and of Wing, list only one
Latin translation—Goulston's, in 1623—during the early part of
the century; there were to be no others before 1700. Two French
translations (1672, 1692) appear in the catalogues of the Bib-
liothèque Nationale, but only the later of these, Dacier's, was
widely enough circulated in England to have found its way to
the British Museum collections. Of course, there was no translation into English. Such negligence does not prove that no one
read *The Poetics,* but it does indicate a lack of interest.[8] The first
and only seventeenth-century critic of importance to expound in
England what might be regarded as a strictly Aristotelian doctrine of tragic functioning was Milton, who in his familiar discussion prefacing *Samson Agonistes* interprets catharsis medi-
cally, as a purgation effected through homeopathic doses of pity

8. A full, if frequently misleading, account of English reactions to *The
Poetics* may be found in Marvin T. Herrick, *The Poetics of Aristotle in
England* (New Haven, 1930), pp. 8–80.

and fear. Milton's countrymen relied on the French academicians for their Aristotle, and most specifically upon Rapin's commentary, translated by Rymer (1674), which made available a firm statement of French Aristotelianism to those Englishmen who had not heard it themselves either as Cromwell's exiles or as hangers-on at Whitehall.

A comparison of Rapin's commentary on the central teleological passage in *The Poetics* with that passage itself will indicate the direction taken by the exegetically orthodox. Aristotle had written: "Tragedy is then, an Imitation of an Action that is Grave, [and] Entire . . . and which without the assistance of Narration, by means of Compassion and Terror perfectly refines in us, all sorts of Passions . . ."[9] Rapin accepts what Aristotle says, interpreting and mingling it with other Aristotelian doctrines:

> [Aristotle] alledges, that *Tragedy* is a *publick Lecture*, without comparison more *instructive* than *Philosophy*; because it teaches the *mind* by the sense, and rectifies the passions by the passions themselves, in calming by their emotion the troubles they excite in the heart. The Philosopher had observ'd two important faults in man to be regulated, *pride*, and *hardness of heart*, and he found for both Vices a cure in *Tragedy*. For it makes man modest, by representing the great *masters of the earth humbled*; and it makes him tender and

9. To present the nature of the Aristotelian text as a seventeenth-century critic would have seen it, I have quoted the passage (vi. 2) from the earliest English translation, *Aristotle's Art of Poetry. Translated from the Original Greek, according to Mr. Theodore Goulston's Edition*, trans. anon. (London, 1705), pp. 69–70. Although this is an English version, corrected according to Goulston's text, of Dacier's French translation, Dacier's original, "achève de purger en nous ces sortes de passions, & toutes les autres semblables," is probably more exact. Cf. Riccoboni's Latin rendering, "per misericordiam, & metum inducens talium perturbationum purgationem."—*Operum Aristotelis Tomi II*, ed I. Casaubon (Aureliae Allobrogum, 1605), II, 505. Dacier's insistence that "purger" means "refine" rather than (as "The Academicks, and afterwards the Stoicks" claimed) *"To drive out, To root them out of the Soul"* (p. 78) authorizes his translator's attempt to find an appropriate English verb less equivocal than "purge."

merciful, by shewing him on the Theatre the strange accidents of life, and the unforeseen disgraces, to which the most
important persons are subject. But because man is naturally
timorous, and compassionate, he may fall into another extreme, to be either too fearful, or too full of pity; the too
much fear may shake the constancy of mind, and the too
great compassion may enfeeble the equity.[10]

Tragedy, Rapin goes on to say, corrects excessive passion by
accustoming the audience to extraordinary scenes of tribulation
and to appeals for compassion: thus tragedy both softens and
hardens by forcing the sensibility to evaluate and respond to
dramatic experience. The generated emotion itself is a moral
agent.

Quite obviously, Rapin has modified Aristotle's notion of plot
in the direction of the moral fable. He has also interpreted
catharsis in line with Christian morality, not only by presenting
a mildly secularized *caritas* as the proper result of the tragic
emotion, but also by introducing a voluntarism which seems
foreign to *The Poetics*. Behind his theory lies the idea of the
moral act, still requiring, as it had for centuries of Platonic and
Christian tradition, at least the consent of the will and the
yielding of obduracy. Thus, despite the affective principles he is
advancing, Rapin appears close to the body of poetics that considers tragedy moral rhetoric, and, in fact, he was a recidivist,
sliding back into a position in which *utile* and *dulce* are two. His
dual position is characteristic of the French and English critics of
the time.[11] Significantly, however, the practical effects of both
the modified Aristotelian position and the fabulism based on

10. René Rapin, *Reflections on Aristotle's Treatise of Poesie. Containing
the necessary, rational, and universal rules for Epick, dramatick, and the other
sorts of poetry* (London, 1674), p. 103.

11. Compare the English translation of Dacier's commentary in *Aristotle's
Art of Poetry* (1705), pp. 78–79, which echoes Rapin's duality. The long life
and significance of Rapin's commentary are suggested by the fact that so late
an author as Richardson, in writing the postscript to *Clarissa,* turns to Rapin
for authority.

Hobbesian-Cartesian rhetorical assumptions were very much the same; the dual position could be maintained without real contradiction, although at the expense of economy. Rapin reasons, from Cartesian principles, that since pity and fear are the strongest and most natural emotions, they are the most agitating and therefore the most pleasurable. Hence they become the most effective *dulcia* available to the tragedian for coating moral lessons.[12] Rapin's attitude, which forces the moral to depend on a hypertrophied emotional vehicle, remains the same whether that vehicle be loaded with didactic fable or with specifics for undecorous passion. It becomes clear, then, why Rapin, having made the Horatian pair one flesh, has so little compunction about parting them asunder. His attitudes and emphases, his mixture of affective and fabulist speculations and his stress on the emotions, may be taken as exemplary of the bulk of late seventeenth-century tragic criticism.

The general position held by Rapin received the support, in England, of Dryden's extraordinary authority: slightly modified, that position dominated English speculation on tragedy for at least the next fifty years. Two essays by Dryden are of particular significance here, the preface to *Troilus and Cressida* (1679) and the complementary "Heads of an answer to Rymer." In the broadest terms, the "Heads" postulate the fabulist, and the *Troilus* preface the affective, position. But, as with Rapin, the empirical implications of the two positions are extremely similar; one has the feeling with both men that the attitude, the knowledge of *quod erat demonstrandum*, was prior to the theory.[13]

12. Rapin, p. 105.

13. The "Heads" were first published from Dryden's jottings on the endpapers of his presentation copy of "Tragedies of the Last Age," when the editor of *The Works of Mr. Francis Beaumont and Mr. John Fletcher* (London, 1711), decided to include them in the introduction to the first volume of the set. Presumably Dryden merely rejected the odd jottings that constitute the "Heads" for the more effective argument that he published as the *Troilus* preface. Cf. Fred Walcott, "John Dryden's Answer to Thomas Rymer's *The Tragedies of the Last Age*," *Philological Quarterly*, XV (1936), 194–214.

In the "Heads," Dryden characteristically speaks of "those Ends of Tragedy, which *Aristotle* and he [Rymer] propose, namely, to cause Terror and Pity."[14] The significance of the chosen infinitive, "to cause," is crucial, for Dryden introduces—or assumes—another version of the same disjunction between the useful and the delightful that fabulist tradition assumed. Aristotle's formulation may be taken to mean that the excitation and the catharsis of pity and fear are both parts of the same process, but Restoration critics did not accept that implication. For them, as for the voluntaristic Rapin, catharsis came as a result of contemplation and will, of meditation on the emotions generated, albeit perhaps a meditation and decision both natural and unconscious. Thus the pleasure of passion separates itself from the bitter moral of passion's fruits. Pragmatically, this division of labor, by which the playwright excited emotions that the spectators' reflections were to temper and apply, led directly to sentiment. By the dictum of Aristotle, the job of Tate or Gildon or Mrs. Pix consisted only in eliciting pity and fear from the audience. Their effectiveness was quantitative, measured by the frequency and the intensity of the tears and sympathetic shudders they evoked. To realize this is to be able to reconcile seeming inconsistencies in Restoration criticism. For example, Gildon's Langbaine claims for Otway "a Tallent, very few of our English Poets have been Master of, in moving the Passions, that are, and ought to be the Aim of all Tragick Poets, Terror and Pity"; while the notice of Mrs. Pix's *Ibrahim,* a few pages later, remarks, "the Distress of *Morena* never fail'd to bring Tears into the Eyes of the Audience . . . , which is the true End of Tragedy."[15] These statements jibe (assuming that "Tears" is a

14. "Heads," sig. A6.
15. Gerard Langbaine, *The Lives and Characters of the English Dramatic Poets. Also an exact account of all the plays that were ever yet printed in the English tongue . . .*, rev. Charles Gildon (London, 1699), sigs. H6, H8. Edward Niles Hooker, in his edition of Dennis (*The Critical Works of John Dennis* [Baltimore, 1939–1943]) quotes Bossuet's puzzled, "Mais laissons, si l'on veut, à Aristote cette manière mystérieuse de les purifier, dont ni lui ni ses

synecdoche) if and only if one realizes that "moving the Passions" means precisely what it says; it is not a shorthand for Aristotle's entire process of excitement and catharsis.

Not only does Dryden interpret the Aristotelian purpose as evocative rather than purgative, he also more or less accepts that purpose in both the "Heads" and the *Troilus* preface, although in each case for different reasons. In the *Troilus* preface, he repeats Rapin's arguments about "softening." Pity and fear are raised, pride and hard-heartedness purged:

> To purge the passions by example, is . . . the particular instruction which belongs to Tragedy. Rapin, a judicious critic, has observed from Aristotle, that pride and want of commiseration are the two most predominant vices in mankind; therefore, to cure us of these two, the inventors of Tragedy have chosen to work upon two other passions, which are fear and pity. We are wrought to fear by their setting before our eyes some terrible example of misfortune, which happened to persons of the highest quality; for such an action demonstrates to us that no condition is privileged from the turns of fortune; this must of necessity cause terror in us, and consequently abate our pride. But when we see that the most virtuous, as well as the greatest, are not exempt from such misfortunes, that consideration moves pity in us, and insensibly works us to be helpful to, and tender over, the distressed; which is the noblest and most god-like of moral virtues.[16]

Dryden goes a bit further than Rapin: he does not talk about rectifying pity and fear ("hardening"), and he is less voluntaristic. But like Rapin's moral standards, Dryden's represent in their emphases—order and degree in the passions, the nurture of

---

interprètes n'ont su encore donner de bonnes raisons" (I, 472). Practicing playwrights did indeed leave catharsis wrapped in philosophic mystery, and turned their hands to those Aristotelian precepts that were most immediately profitable to them.

16. *Essays of John Dryden*, ed. W. P. Ker, 2 vols. (New York, 1961), I, 208–209. Hereafter these volumes will be cited as "Ker."

benevolence—a reasonably common late seventeenth-century editing of Christian doctrine. The road to those moral standards was that of emotion.

In the "Heads," Dryden offers a different rationale for the passions, while trying to skirt Rymer's strict "poetical justice." He answers Rymer's insistence on the objective nature of the fable by referring instructive value to the audience's response, and thus to the evocation of morally functional emotion: "[Not] only Pity and Terror are to be mov'd as the only Means to bring us to Virtue, but generally Love to Virtue, and Hatred to Vice, by shewing the Rewards of one and Punishments of the other; at least by rendring Virtue always amiable, though it be shown unfortunate; and Vice detestable, tho' it be shown Triumphant."[17] By implication, Dryden admits any dramatic technique, empirically tested, which has a moral effect, while he passes over Rymer's quasi-theological ends involving a display of Providence. To specify what the dramatist must show imposes a limitation on technique which Dryden was disinclined to accept. Thus in the "Heads" as in the *Troilus* preface, he postulates purely social and ethical ends depending upon psychological effect. Virtue now receives its rewards not because God loves it and cherishes it, but because the pit and boxes do. Without discarding fabulist theories, then, the "Heads" alter the fable from a demonstration of heavenly dispensation to an evocation of ethical feeling. The affective *Troilus* preface also demanded ethical feelings, specifically pity and fear. In both essays, profit and pleasure lay in emotional response; and a *rapprochement* between Dryden's Aristotle and Dryden's Horace was the harmonious result.

The authorization for what I have called "serial drama" proceeded logically from the position of either the "Heads" or the *Troilus* preface. The depreciation of the plot, which had enjoyed a necessary predominance in traditional fabulist theory, led directly to emphasis on parts instead of the whole, and, in particu-

17. "Heads," sig. A8. See the discussion by Baxter Hathaway, "John Dryden and the Function of Tragedy," *PMLA*, LVIII (1943), 665–673.

lar, emphasis on characters. Rapin had said that "it is not the admirable Intrigue, the surprising and wonderful Events, the extraordinary Incidents that make the Beauty of a *Tragedy;* it is the Discourses when they are *Natural* and *Passionate.*"[18] It would be misguided to take this as a plea for finer dramatic poetry: "nature" and "passion" are, as I shall suggest, connected with the pathetic character. For the moment, it is enough to observe that Rapin's animadversions strike at both the theories of tragic pleasure which had preceded the Hobbesian and Cartesian hypotheses: demonstrations of Providence are not even mentioned, while the significant pleasures of artistry are specifically denied. The same attitude is implicit in Dryden, who explains in the "Heads" that Aristotle "places the Fable first; not *quoad dignitatem, sed quoad fundamentum.*"[19] Empathy with characters through the nature and passion of their discourses, a mere rhetorical appurtenance to earlier critics, now assumes equal or greater utilitarian significance than the plot, because equally or more emotionally stirring.

Natural passionate speeches, moments of great affective incision, require empathy with the speaker: if the speeches are to be the foci of the play, the characters must be stressed and developed. Therefore, both Dryden and Rapin laid emphasis on the principle of "concernment." "Concernment" begins with the chapter of Aristotle's *Poetics* (xiii.4) in which Aristotle says that pity is evoked by undeserved misfortune, and fear by the plight of a man like ourselves. This may be interpreted so as to postulate a relationship either between the spectator and the situation or between the spectator and the characters. Corneille provides an illustration for the former: "La pitié d'un malheur où nous voyons tomber nos semblables nous porte à la crainte d'un pareil pour nous; cette crainte, au désir de l'éviter; et ce désir, à purger, modèrer, rectifier, et même déraciner en nous le passion qui

18. Rapin, p. 116.
19. "Heads," sig. A6.

plonge à nos yeux dans ce malheur les personnes que nous plaignons, par cette raison commune, mais naturelle et indubitable, que pour éviter l'effet il faut retrancher la cause."[20] In this passage, Corneille conceives of pity and fear as reciprocal functions which repel the spectator from his own dangerous passions. The audience responds to the situation, to the plot.

This kind of statement may be compared to the affective statements of Dryden and Rapin. While Corneille here treats pity and fear only as means, Dryden and Rapin, the latter somewhat gingerly, accept pity and fear as themselves constituting much of the moral purpose of the play. In the one, the audience is to react to the universalized situation; in the other, pity and fear, now differentiated in identity and function, bloom from particular instances, from specific and self-contained "undeserved misfortunes" as well as—perhaps rather than—the fable's moral implications. Rapin, beginning with the Cartesian theory of tragic pleasure, reasons that without "the agitation of the Soul mov'd by the Passions[,] *Tragedy* cannot be delightful to the Spectator . . . , he must *enter* into all the different thoughts of the Actors, interest himself in their Adventures, *fear, hope, afflict* himself, and *rejoyce* with them."[21] Dryden repeats this argument in the *Troilus* preface (Ker, I, 211); and in the "Heads," proposes a further rationale for concernment, that characters of varying moral qualities could exert the proper emotional appeal or repulsion thereby: "If then the Encouragement of Virtue, and Discouragement of Vice, be the proper End of Poetry in Tragedy: Pity and Terror, tho' good Means, are not the only: For all the Passions in their turns are to be set in Ferment; as Joy, Anger, Love, Fear, are to be used as the Poet[']s common Places; and a general Concernment for the principal Actors is to be rais'd, by making them appear such in their

20. Pierre Corneille, "Discours de la tragédie . . . ," *Oeuvres,* ed. Ch. Marty-Laveaux, 12 vols. (Paris, 1862–1868), I, 53.
21. Rapin, p. 105.

Characters, their Words and Actions, as will Interest the Audience in their Fortunes."[22] Quite obviously, this attitude of Rapin's and Dryden's differs from traditional fabulist attitudes in stress, in degree, in intensity, in tone; not in kind. The same thing is true of most of the other new principles they put forth. None the less, the subversion of tradition is clear. To furnish one's theories with concernment was to welcome the drama of passion. Furthermore, if the new criticism had removed ancient restraints upon tragic technique, concernment replaced them with new requirements. Playwrights quickly realized, for example, that burghers in the boxes would weep best and most freely for the *petites angoisses* of burghers on the stage. Domestic tragedy began its long stand here.

Dryden's position, with its implications, defined the suppositions of tragic theorists for the next half-century. His most important immediate successor, John Dennis, began under the influence of Dacier, stressing emotional austerity and didactic fable as the contributions of tragedy to instilling virtue; but Dennis' later criticism goes on to include "softening" and also the necessity of "concernment," the latter because "the greater the Resemblance is between him who suffers, and him who commiserates, the stronger will the Apprehension, and consequently, the Compassion be."[23] When Dennis, by accepting the direct moral function of emotional response and the emphasis on character, had adopted a position roughly similar to Dryden's, no important critic in England remained in opposition to emotional, or "sentimental," tragedy. Wasserman remarks, "That the major function of a tragedy is to produce some kind of beneficial effect upon the spectator through the excitation of pity and fear, was, of course,

22. "Heads," sigs. A8, A8ᵛ.
23. *Critical Works of John Dennis*, I, 128. One can see Dennis' changing attitude by comparing the essays of the early 1690's with the answer he gave Collier in *The Usefulness of the Stage* (1698). His original strict adherence to Dacier, such as is found in *The Impartial Critick* (e.g., *Critical Works*, I, 33–35), differs startlingly from his position of a very few years later.

the central tenet of eighteenth-century dramatic theory."[24] The ideal of tragic success is expressed in Bevill Higgons' prologue to George Granville's *The Jew of Venice* (1701), in which Shakespeare's ghost compliments Dryden:

> Whose stupid Souls thy Passion cannot move,
> Are deaf indeed to Nature and to Love.
> When thy *Aegyptian* weeps, what Eyes are dry!
> Or who can live to see thy *Roman* dye.

Charles Johnson, in the dedication to *The Force of Friendship* (1710), speaks of the supporters of tragedy as persons of sentiment and sensibility, not of moral gravity: ". . . where indeed can expiring Tragedy hope for Countenance and Patronage but from those few, very few elegant Spirits who are pleas'd with the Distress of a well wrought Scene, who with the utmost Indulgence to their Reason, behold the Conduct of our Passions on the Stage, and with a generous Sympathy feel alternate Joy and Pain, when Virtue either conquers, or is contending with adverse Fate" (A2, A2ᵛ).[25] "Generous Sympathy" and "alternate Joy and Pain" were the standards of the new tragedy. Dr. Towne's prologue to William Hunt's *The Fall of Tarquin* (1713) holds up the same standards:

> Oft have the pleas'd Spectators view'd each Scene,
> And felt the varying Passions Throb within,
> With pitying Eyes beheld the Hero bleed,
> Or joy'd to see the buskin'd Captive freed.

24. Wasserman, "Pleasures of Tragedy," p. 283.
25. Northrop Frye, *The Well-Tempered Critic* (Bloomington, 1963), remarks, p. 123, that "we occasionally hear of people who faint or scream at plays: this is always interpreted as a tribute to the vividness of the play, not to their critical sensitivity." Yet Johnson's position, although it does call for some aesthetic discernment, relies heavily on immediate emotional reaction, empathetic tears that do demonstrate (for Johnson) "critical sensitivity." The extremity of such an attitude demonstrates strikingly how far "vividness" of a certain sort had become the measure of merit, and thus how far taste had become a matter of emotional receptivity rather than reasonable judgment.

It seemed clear that these emotions were profitable other than as sources of sentimental pleasure; in what their profit lay was less clear. James Wright, in the 1690's, follows Dryden's "Heads" (although he was not, of course, influenced by them) in assuming that the emotions reinforce moral values: he asserts that tragedy leads to a "Reformation of Manners" because it "carries something of Terrour against those who are Great and Wicked, and Raises Compassion for the Sufferings of Good Men."[26] Edward Filmer, writing a few years later, is in agreement, although he shunts terror aside in favor of pity:

> Tragedy indeed does raise the Passions; and its chief work is to raise *Compassion:* For the Great Entertainment of Tragedy, is the moving of that tenderest and noblest Humane Passion, *Pity.* And what is it we pity there, but the Distresses, Calamities and Ruins of *Honour, Loyalty, Fidelity* or *Love,* &c. represented in some True or Fictitious, Historick or Romantick Subject of the Play. Thus *Virtue,* like *Religion* by its *Martyrdom,* is rendered more shining by its sufferings, and the Impression we receive from *Tragedy,* is only making us in Love with *Virtue,* (for Pity is a little Kin to Love) . . .[27]

Quite closely related to these positions resembling that enunciated in the "Heads" is the praise of compassion for its own sake, as in the *Troilus* preface. Nicholas Rowe's definition of tragic pity in the preface to *The Ambitious Step-Mother* (1701) as "a sort of regret proceeding from good nature" (A3) indicates the benevolist philosophy which at times underlay the exaltation of the sympathetic heart in the theatre. "The End of Tragedy,"

26. [James Wright], *Country Conversations: Being an account of some discourses that happen'd in a visit to the country last summer, on divers subjects; chiefly of the modern comedies, . . . of translated verse, . . . of poets and poetry* (London, 1694), p. 10.

27. Edward Filmer, *A Defence of Dramatick Poetry: being a review of Mr. Collier's View of the Immorality and Profaneness of the Stage* (London, 1698), p. 71.

wrote Gay in his preface to *The What D'Ye Call It* (1715),
". . . [is] to show human Life in its Distresses, Imperfections,
and Infirmities, thereby to soften the Mind of Man from its
natural Obduracy and Haughtiness . . ." (A2ʳ). A little later in
the century, John Mottley's prologues to his *The Imperial Cap-
tives* (1720) and *Antiochus* (1721) discourse on virtuous griefs
and generous passions.

As we have seen, the practical results, or at least concomitants,
of such criticism were that tragedy became more "natural" and
more domestic. The passions in drama were associated with
"nature." Thus Addison writes that "Otway has followed nature
in the language of his tragedy, and therefore shines in the
passionate parts, more than any of our English poets," while
Steele attributes true tragic passion, not to pomp, but to "something of a plain and simple nature which breaks in on our souls.
. . ."[28] Universalized or moralized characters of high degree
began, very slowly, to be supplanted by more particularized
characters conceived psychologically. Immediacy of appeal
meant a lowering of tone. For example, Henry Mestayer's prologue to his *The Perfidious Brother* (1716) explains:

> To move each gen'rous Heart, and draw your Tears,
> In Artless Dress the Tragic Muse appears:
> Stript of her Regal Pomp, and glitt'ring Show,
> She represents a Tale of private Woe.

Aaron Hill's prologue to James Mitchell's *The Fatal Extravagance* (1721) epitomizes the idea of domesticity with handsome
clarity:

> To Ills, remote from our Domestic Fears,
> We lend our Wonder, but with-hold our Tears.
> Not so, when, from such Passions, as our own,
> Some Favourite Folly's dreadful Fate is shown;

28. Joseph Addison and Richard Steele, *The Spectator*, ed. George A.
Aitken, 8 vols. (London, 1898), No. 39, I, 203. Richard Steele *et al.*, *The
Tatler*, ed. George A. Aitken, 4 vols. (London, 1898), No. 68, II, 140.

There the Soul bleeds, for what it feels within;
And conscious Pity shakes at suffering Sin.

Two general lines of thought have been traced in the criticism of the seventeenth and early eighteenth centuries. The first, what has been called the "fabulist" hypothesis, held that the value of a play is in the moral of its story; but fabulism was subverted through the necessity of the play's giving pleasure to make its moral operative. The connection of the experience of passion with theatrical pleasure was the result of the Cartesian physiology which gave a rational basis to Addison's empirical observation that "terror and commiseration leave a pleasing anguish in the mind."[29] Furthermore, some critics held that the moral of the fable demanded active reinforcement from the passions, and the moral itself was made the emotional response of loving virtue and hating vice rather than the more "reasonable" realization of God's Providence. The second line of thought, what has been called the "affective" hypothesis, interpreted Aristotle to support the idea that the exercise of the passions, especially those of pity and fear, was itself a desideratum. The path between such a theory and emotional or "sentimental" drama is quite obvious.

Both the fabulist and affective hypotheses, then, led to the same end; and, in fact, critics whose general attitude toward

29. Addison's comment, in *The Spectator*, No. 40, forms part of his argument for affective tragedy rather than that "reformed according to the chymerical Notion of Poetical Justice." It would be interesting to know the relative influences of tragic theory and of Locke in bringing to Addison's aesthetics—codified in "The Pleasures of the Imagination"—the affective bias for which Locke has often been credited. I suspect that the congenial Locke was more valuable in this literary matter as the source of explanatory terminology than as the source of ideas already current in criticism. If as Elioseff remarks, "Addison's importance to the history of English criticism lies in his simultaneous adherence to the principles of 'mimetic-formal' criticism and his formulation of the first coherent statement of affective literary theory in English literary criticism," Addison is principally making a generic extension of the attitudes outlined above. (Lee Andrew Elioseff, *The Cultural Milieu of Addison's Literary Criticism* [Austin, Texas, 1963], p. 10.)

tragedy was consistent managed to maintain both of them. The most important of these men was Dryden, whose *Troilus* preface and "Heads of an answer to Rymer," taken together, anticipate every significant development in tragic theory for at least the next forty or fifty years. The main changes, as usual, were changes in emphasis. Although a copious number of early eighteenth-century critics reiterated the fabulist theories, both stress and interest were primarily and pragmatically upon the exciting of emotion. And it was eliciting emotion which was to prove the central concern of the eighteenth-century playwright, as well as of his nineteenth- and twentieth-century successors.

For the purposes of trying to understand the process of change in late seventeenth-century tragedy, the pattern of this criticism is as important as its conclusions. One finds the same kind of introspection and ad hoc rationalization in the writing of the plays as in the writing about them. Here too, as in almost all the Restoration's use of the ancients, one can see the flexibility of English "classicism," in which the "rules" mask a compromise between the empirically successful and the intellectually true. While the balance between the two elements of this compromise shifted over the course of years, neither was (or should have been) neglected in the creation of literature and of literary theory. Nothing seems more foolish than the modern procedure of denouncing the Restoration for its rigid archaism on the one hand and its distortion of the classics on the other, when in fact its eclectic synthesis of critical attitudes turned out to be both creative and intelligent. Similarly, the plays that we are about to consider are synthetic, experimental, and also creative and intelligent at their best.

2

THE ATTACK UPON
HEROICS

WHILE THE THEORETICAL CRITICS WERE REVISING THE CANONS of tragedy as we have just seen, practical critics were trying to curb the taste of the town for heroic plays, and to prove that, as Francis Fane's prologue to his *Love in the Dark* (1675) announces:

> Rhyme is a cheating Vapour, which unseen,
> Ill Poets, like ill Spirits, pass between,
> To good Wits but a shade, to bad a Skreen.

This unofficial campaign assumed great importance in seventeenth-century dramatic history, since its presuppositions later became norms of taste, tying in directly with the tragic theory that we have just discussed.

Edward Ravenscroft, in the prologue to *The Citizen Turn'd Gentleman* (1672), commented wryly on the popularity of heroics; of

> . . . the great Heroes now
> In Playes of Rhyme and Noyse with wond'rous show.
> Then shall the House (to see these Hectors kill and slay,
> That bravely fight out the whole plot of th' Play,)
> Be for at least six months full ev'ry day.   (A3ᵛ)

Heroic verse, wrote Dryden in the same year, is "already in possession of the stage; and I dare confidently affirm, that very few tragedies, in this age, shall be received without it" (Ker, I, 148). "This age" was short-lived. By the end of the decade, eight years after Dryden's declaration, the heroic play was dead. The dwindling of the playwrights' interest in licking new heroics into shape and of the public's interest in acclaiming them can, even without full statistics on repertory, be clearly indicated. Avery, for instance, mentions only five performances of rhymed tragedies after 1680; and of those, four are of the chaster, earlier *The Indian-Queen* and *The Tragedy of Mustapha*. Forty-two plays in couplets, according to Nicoll, can be assigned to the twenty years from the Restoration to 1680; to the following twenty years, five.[1] Stage histories of individual rhymed plays detail, by their thinness, the sudden falling-off.[2] So do acting records. Mrs. Barry, who began her long career in 1675, may have been trained by Rochester for the Hungarian Queen Isabella in *Mustapha*, but she appears to have had little chance to play such roles: of the 118 known roles she assumed, only two were in rhymed tragedy, one of them the bit part in which she made her debut, that of Draxilla in Otway's *Alcibiades* (1675). William

1. Emmett L. Avery, "A Tentative Calendar of Daily Theatrical Performances, 1660–1700," *Research Studies of the State College of Washington*, XIII (1945), 225–283. Allardyce Nicoll, *A History of English Drama, 1660–1900*, Vol. I, *Restoration Drama, 1660–1700* (4th ed., Cambridge, 1952), p. 100. Only one of these plays, Nicoll points out, dates from the 1680's.

2. The evidence of repertory is scanty; what there is of it supports these assertions. For example, Boyle's *Tryphon* seems to have had no revivals before 1700. The same holds for Lee's *Nero* and *Gloriana*. *Sophonisba* was revived in Oxford in 1680 or 1681; Lee's editors claim that "the play continued popular for almost a century" but present no evidence for its having been performed between 1680 and 1700. Montague Summers, in his editions of Dryden and of Otway, assures the reader of the popularity of *The Conquest of Granada* and *Aureng-Zebe*, but presents no specific evidence of any production from 1680 to 1700; he mentions revivals of *Tyrannick Love* in 1686 and 1694, and of *Alcibiades* in 1687, but does not oblige the curious with his sources. Whatever those sources may be, they do not include either Nicoll or Genest's standard *Some Account of the English Stage*, 10 vols. (1832). He also mentions, but does not locate, a letter from Barton Booth to Aaron Hill claiming that *Don Carlos* drew better than either *The Orphan* or *Venice Preserv'd*. See *The Dramatic Works of Roger Boyle, Earl of Orrery*, ed. W. S. Clark, 2 vols. (Cambridge, Mass., 1937); *The Works of Nathaniel Lee*, ed. Thomas B. Stroup and Arthur L. Cooke, 2 vols. (New Brunswick, N.J., 1954–1955); *The Dramatic Works of John Dryden*, ed. Montague Summers, 6 vols. (London, 1931–1932), II, 328, III, 13–14, IV, 77; *The Complete Works of Thomas Otway*, ed. Montague Summers, 3 vols. (London, 1926), I, 48, 71.

Mountfort, who began his career in 1678, never, as far as is known, played in rhymed tragedy.[3] By the eighteenth century, the aversion to dramatic rhyme, despite a few glimmerings of favor about 1700, was such that even Shakespeare's couplets and stanzas were disapproved of and cut by adapters.[4]

These facts may well suggest a more extreme decline in the popularity of heroics than was actually the case: information is more likely to be available about new plays than about revivals, and complaints about rhymed plays—indicative of continuing rankling—continue throughout the century. Furthermore, the seventh edition of Buckingham's *The Rehearsal*, published in 1701 "As it is now Acted at the Theatre-Royal," presents substantially the same biting jests and burlesque as does the first edition, evidently without fear that topical satire on the heroic play was in any way outdated. But even if the figures exaggerate, they do not lie.

The reasons for the public *volte-face* are unclear, and, as usual complex. The simplest answer is that playgoers were surfeited with heroics. Mrs. Behn declares in the prologue to *The Emperor of the Moon* (1687), looking back over past years:

> Long, and at vast Expence the industrious Stage
> Has strove to please a dull ungrateful Age:
> With Heroes and with Gods we first began,
> And thunder'd to you in Heroick Strain:
> Some dying Love-sick Queen each Night you injoy'd,
> And with Magnificence at last were cloy'd: . . .
> So Spark in an Intrigue of Quality,

3. Mrs. Barry's dramatic training is mentioned in *The History of the English Stage* (London, 1741) nominally by Betterton, p. 15. Her repertory is listed by John Harold Wilson, *All the King's Ladies* (Chicago, 1958), pp. 110–117. Mountfort's career is traced by Albert S. Borgman in *The Life and Death of William Mountfort* (Cambridge, Mass., 1935), pp. 1–120 *passim*.

4. George Branam, *Eighteenth Century Adaptations of Shakespearean Tragedy* (Berkeley, 1956), p. 45.

Grows weary of his splendid Drudgery;
Hates the Fatigue, and cries a Pox upon her,
What a damn'd bustle's here with Love and Honour.[5]

However, "Astraea" miscalculated the audience's appetite for magnificent sweets. English opera, lavish with effects and machines, grew in popularity as the century wore on, illustrating "the victory of sugar over diabetes"[6]—if indeed the public had ever been ailing. No evidence indicates that theatrical splendors, supernatural show, or love among royalty ever displeased the Restoration. Nor did the public tire of the "damn'd bustle" with love and honor, as the appeal of *All for Love, Venice Preserv'd,* and *The Rival Queens* attests. To ascertain the reasons for the disappearance of the heroic play, and therefore for the transfusion of energy and talents into unrhymed tragedy, one must go back to the seventeenth-century criticisms of the rhymed plays themselves.

The unpopularity of rhyme, of course, was not a sudden fever of the theatrical sensibility in the late 1670's. The preface to the anonymous *Emilia* refers to the controversy as widespread in 1672, and humbly retires from it:

> The *Writing* or *Language,* I have accomodated to the Persons, *Verse;* [sic] for the more *Heroick,* and *Prose,* for the rest, with often allay of this with the other, to make it more flexible, which else would be too stiff.
>
> For the *Rhyme,* which is onely the finishing of our *Verse,* and which our English Ears by Custom do so expect, as they will scarcely allow *Verses* to be compleat without it, I will not commend it, because it has so many Potent

5. *The Works of Aphra Behn,* ed. Montague Summers, 6 vols. (London, 1913), III, 393.

6. I am indebted to George Jean Nathan for the quip; he applied it to Barrie. F. C. Brown, in his biography of Settle (Chicago, 1910), suggests that Settle's skill in contriving machinery was the cause of Betterton's interest in him in the last decade of the century. Everything *but* the technique of splendor had disappeared, in other words.

Enemies; nor condemn it, because it has so many Potent
Friends, but leave it to others judgments, as I do all the
rest.   (A2ʳ)

In the same year, Crowne's prologue to *The History of Charles
the Eighth of France* apologizes for his rhyme, and he begins the
epilogue (L3ʳ), "With how much patience have you heard to
day / The whining noise of a dull Rhiming Play?" And Crowne
remarks in dedicating this tragedy to Rochester that "the enemies
it ha's already met with have been fewer, then a Play in Verse
. . . could expect; considering how many there are, that exclaim
against Rhime, though never so well writ" (a). By 1677, the wits
and "Criticks" must have appeared less patient: the epilogue to
the first part of *The Destruction of Jerusalem* promises

> . . . all you Wits, who for some secret Crime,
> Have taken up a pique against poor Rhime,
> And you at present are no little store . . .
> First for his Rhime he [the poet] pardon does implore,
> And promises to ring those Chimes no more.   (H4ʳ)

Except for *Caligula* (1698), written while he was recuperating
from a fit of delirium, Crowne kept his promise; and was
strengthened in his recantation by that of Settle in the same
year. Both men were trailing the sagacious Dryden, who had
abandoned rhyme after *Aureng-Zebe*, a season earlier.[7]

---

7. Nicoll, *Restoration Drama*, p. 86, quotes Settle's depreciatory epilogue to
Ibrahim (1677; produced *ca.* March 1676) beginning: "How many has our
Rhimer kill'd to day? / What need of *Siege* and *Conquest* in a Play, / When
Love can do the work as well as they." The playful self-scorn of "Rhimer" is
intensified in the prologue to *Pastor Fido*, nine months later, in which Settle
refers to the current disrepute of "the dull Rhiming Fops of the Last Age."
The epilogue (K2) attributes the death of rhyme to mere fashion, grown
contemptible through familiarity and lowering of decorum:

> Rhiming, which once had got so much your passion,
> When it became the Lumber of the Nation,
> Like Vests, your Seaven years Love, grew out of fashion.
> Great Subjects, and Grave Poets please no more:

When one turns to the criticism which occasioned the change, one finds that most of it is casual, probably reflecting the sneers and witticisms of the coffee-house critics, who had more interest in expressions of distaste than in polished codifications. For example, the prologue to the anonymous *The Woman Turn'd Bully* (1675) begins (A2ʳ) with a comparison of "Heroick Rattle" to "a graceless child"; or the anonymous poem "The Laureat" describes Dryden's heroics:

> Here 'twas thou mad'st the Bells of Fancy Chime,
> And choak'd the Town with suffocating Rhime . . .
> Flush'd with Success, full Gallery and Pit,
> Thou bravest all Mankind with want of Wit . . .
> But when the Men of Sense thy Error saw,
> They check'd thy Muse, and kept the Termagant in awe.[8]

Or William Joyner warns the reader of his *The Roman Empress* (1671) that "such who expect to have their ears tickled with the gingling Antitheses of Love and Honor, and such like petty wares, will find themselves deceiv'd" (A3). However, many of the criticisms are more satisfyingly specific.

The simplest attack on rhyme is that which protests the mere sound of the words. Milton, for instance, writes that "our best English Tragedies [have rejected rhyme] as a thing of itself, to all judicious ears, triveal and of no true musical delight; which consists onely in apt Numbers, fit quantity of Syllables, and the sense variously drawn out from one Verse into another, not in the jingling sound of like endings, a fault avoyded by the learned Ancients . . ."[9] Similar aural displeasure is expressed by the

---

> Their high strains now to humble Farce must lower
> . . . as with Habits [i.e., garb], so 'tis with the Stage.
> Fashion is all the Beauty of the Age.

8. *State Poems; continued from the time of O. Cromwel, to the year 1697* (1697), Kᵛ.

9. Preface to *Paradise Lost*, *The Works of John Milton*, ed. Frank A. Patterson *et al.*, 18 vols. (New York, 1931–1938), II, Part I, p. 6. Morris Freedman, "Milton and Dryden on Rhyme," *Huntington Library Quarterly*,

author of the "Preface to the Reader" before *The Successfull Straingers* (1690), who describes Mountfort's style: "like soft *Waller's* verse, thy Prose does show; / Harmonious is the sound, tunes every Line, / More pleasing far, then Gingling tiresome Rhime" (A4ʳ). Such feelings, although they may be profoundly important in stimulating a taste or distaste for some artistic device as the sensibility is either charmed or nagged, do not yield to analysis. Objections based wholly on the actual sound of the spoken line are relatively rare at the time; and one would suspect that an ear that had been trained to the couplet would find it intrinsically as comfortable to listen to as blank verse or prose. In other words, physiological objections would *diminish* with the settling in of habit and expectation. But until faint aural distresses can be gauged more accurately than they now are, the problem will remain moot. For the Restoration, of course, it must always remain moot.[10]

XXIV (1961), 337–344, advances some evidence to support his contention that Milton's comments were a response to the Dryden-Howard controversy. This contention is, perhaps, further strengthened by Marvell's possible reference to the controversy in his laudatory poem on *Paradise Lost:* "Well mightst thou scorn thy Readers to allure / With tinkling Rhime, of thy own Sense secure; / While the *Town-Bays* writes all the while and spells, ..."—*The Poems and Letters of Andrew Marvell,* ed. H. M. Margoliouth, 2 vols. (2nd ed., Oxford, 1952), I, 132. See also H. J. Oliver, *Sir Robert Howard (1626–1698)* (Durham, N.C., 1963), pp. 114–116.

10. On these purely aesthetic grounds, a defense was made by Thomas Shipman before his *Henry the Third of France* (1678; produced 1672):

> Let any man suppose a *representation* of some considerable length, to be perform'd in short sentences, and of unequal cadances, one cannot fancy any thing to be more wearisome. But when it runs in equal *Measures,* neither so at length to stretch the sinews of *Discourse* and Fancy, as upon a Rack, nor so short as to cramp 'em; but sizable both to the speaker and hearer, it must needs advance the satisfaction of both Parties, together with the reputation of the Poet. [Classical poets did not use rhyme, but in English, descended from the early tongues of the bards and druids, it is natural and spirited.] For I refer it to any ingenious rational person, that can write or Judge, what briskness is infused into any fit Subject by a well-ordered and an unforced *Rhime* . . . I am not here to answer

Far more interesting is the frequent criticism that rhyme banishes sense from the stage, a criticism based on the old antithesis between rhyme and reason. Both practically and theoretically the two often appeared mutually exclusive. A good number of comments have come down to the present indicating that rhyme on stage hindered the sense of the lines from coming through. Samuel Pepys, for instance, saw " 'The Indian Queene' acted; which indeed is a most pleasant show, and beyond my expectation; the play good, but spoiled with the ryme, which breaks the sense."[11] Further criticisms take on a more acerb tone, from St. Serfe's *Tarugo's Wiles* (1668)—

> [*The poets man takes out a Rattle and whirles it about his head.*
>
> *Play.* 'Slife, I think this Prose Poets fancy will take; for if I be not mistaken, a Rattle will be better understood by a great many here then the best kind of Rhyme
>
> (Prologue, A4)

—to the bluntness of "*A Lenten* Prologue *refus'd by the* Players, 1682," which charges that "gingling Rhime for Reason here you swallow; / Like *Orpheus* Musick makes Beasts to follow,"[12] and

---

for bald *Rhimes*, that serve only to make bad sense worse, I speak of easie smooth *Rhime* in *Verse,* such as exalts *Sense* and makes it *Rapture* . . . And a *Speech* on the *Stage* (be its Concerns what it will) must be far more harmonious and pleasing in *Rhime,* and more congenial to the Soul.   (A4, A4ᵛ)

It still gave Cavendish's Lady Haughty (*The Triumphant Widow:* 1677; produced 1674) a "head ake" (I2; Act IV).

11. *The Diary of Samuel Pepys,* ed. H. B. Wheatley, 8 vols. (London, 1926), IV, 27 (February 1, 1663/4).

12. *State Poems* (1697), L5ᵛ. Here are some examples of similar criticism between St. Serfe and the *"Lenten* Prologue." In *The Reformation* (1673), the prologue (*2) includes: "[The poet] ha's not left us Room for Gaudy Scene; / Which uses to amuse you for a time, / Whilst Nonsense safely glides away in Rime." In *The Triumphant Widow,* the Musician declares, "Come, Sir, go on, I love Tragedy, especially Heroick, Oh, it does chime, and make the finest noise, 'tis no matter whether it be sense or no, so it be Heroick" (G3ᵛ; Act III). "Advice to Apollo" (in *Poems on Affairs of State* [3rd ed., 1699], O4ᵛ), a poem of 1678, says that Dryden's satire is so bad that "H'had

Lacy's epilogue to *Sir Hercules Buffoon* (1684), accusing the audience of being

> Meer Epicures in Thinking; and in fine,
> As difficult to please in Plays as Wine:
> . . . some forsooth
> Love *Rhenish Wine* and *Sugar;* Plays in meeter;
> Like dead Wine, swallowing Nonsense Rhimes make *sweeter*.
>
> (H3)

These last criticisms, and also Dryden's (see note 12), have the energy of distrust behind them: they view rhyme as an opiate of sorts, an agent of fanciful and obscurantist delusion. As Rymer puts it in his *Short View*, opposing the French use of rhyme: "Our Ear shou'd not be hankering after the Ryme, when the business should wholly take us up, and fill our Head. The words must be all free, independent, and disengag'd, no entanglement of Ryme to be in our way. We must clear the Decks, and down with the Ornaments and Trappings in the day of Action, and Engagement."[13] And rhyme indeed seems to have substituted sound for sense. When Colley Cibber talks about the powerful effect of Betterton's rant from a rhymed portion of *The Rival*

better make *Almanzor* give offence / In fifty Lines without one word of Sense." And Dryden himself, in his prologue to *The Loyal General* (1680), accuses the audience of being able to digest only the weakest pabulum: "A Meal of Tragedy wou'd make ye Sick / Unless it were a very tender Chick. / Some Scenes in Sippets wou'd be worth our time, / Those wou'd go down; some Love that's poach'd in Rime . . ."

13. *Critical Works*, p. 118. As an illustration of the ease of finding rationalizations for one's own work, one might note that Rymer's "Advertisement" to his rhymed tragedy *Edgar* (1678) contains a cautious recommendation of dramatic rhyme (*Critical Works*, p. 77).

The brisk dismissal of ornament, including rhyme, is integral with the growing annoyance about eloquence of all sorts, homiletic and expository as well as dramatic, which scholars such as R. F. Jones have so lengthily detailed. Donald Bond's "'Distrust' of Imagination in English Neo-Classicism," *PQ*, XIV (1935), 54–69, is also suggestive. Any number of related attitudes ramify from the straitened and clarified temperament which was gaining a greater hold throughout the period, and the study of each of them adds to the historical sympathy for the others.

Queens, he stresses the emotional incision, not of Lee's verse, but of the melody, the sheer sound: "When these flowing Numbers came from the Mouth of a *Betterton* the Multitude no more desired sense to them than our musical *Connoisseurs* think it essential in the celebrate Airs of an *Italian* Opera. Does not this prove that there is very near as much Enchantment in the well-govern'd Voice of an Actor as in the sweet Pipe of an Eunuch?"[14]

If the serious theatre was to have more reason and philosophic weight than the sensuous abandonments of the opera, replacing form with ornament, *ratio* with *sensus,* was intolerable. But, of course, the heroic play demanded ornament to achieve admiration; and this includes verbal as well as scenic ornament. Thus heroic organization on the principle that "sound, as well as sense, perswades,"[15] was to become more and more unpalatable to the age; furthermore, a principle which allotted to sound its own share and behests thereby forced compromises between rhyme and reason. Certainly, in most individual instances, these compromises could be settled. But the point cannot be overemphasized that the thrust of the dialectic which spurns rhyme and exalts reason is a thrust away from heroics in general, actually and ideally, and not merely away from the particular immediate offender, the dramatic couplet.

Like the objections to the sound of heroic plays, the attack on ornament (including rhyme) concentrated on detailed style; but its implications were more sweeping, since it proceeded from an aesthetic posture rather than from an isolated physiological unease. This aesthetic posture, explicitly broad in its condemnation, was fully articulated by the critics. Its burden was that the heroic play, with its rhymed speech, heroic hero, plumy helmets, and rhetorical emotion, was a freak, a burlesque of nature. A

14. *An Apology for the Life of Mr. Colley Cibber* . . . , ed. Robert W. Lowe, 2 vols. (London, 1889), I, 106.

15. The formula is Waller's, from his epilogue to his posthumously published version of *The Maid's Tragedy.*

typical criticism of diction from this point of view is the Earl of Mulgrave's:

> *Figures* of *Speech*, which Poets think so fine,
> Art's needless Varnish to make Nature shine,
> Are all but Paint upon a beauteous Face,
> And in Descriptions only claim a place.
> But to make Rage declame, and Grief discourse,
> From Lovers in despair fine things to force,
> Must needs succeed, for who can chuse but pity
> To see poor Hero's miserably witty?
> But O the Dialogues, where jest and mock
> Is held up like a rest at Shittle-cock!
> Or else like Bells eternally they Chime,
> Men dye in Simile, and live in Rime.[16]

The most thoroughly inclusive of such criticisms is Buckingham's *The Rehearsal*.

Dryden and Sir Robert Howard, disputing the propriety of rhyme in the mid-1660's, were among the first critics to bruit this argument. Dryden, dedicating *The Rival Ladies* (1664) to Boyle, chose to defend rhyme, first by demonstrating precedents for its use and then by expounding its practical advantages. He makes three points of particular interest here: he tries to show rhyme subservient to reason, natural in style, decorous in proper application. Critics, he says, have objected that "rhyme is only an embroidery of sense, to make that which is ordinary in itself, pass for excellent with less examination." Dryden counters that the difficulty of writing natural rhymed verse forces careful and judicious purgation of "luxuriant" fancy, thereby fining the poet's stock of all but the "richest and clearest thoughts." That the rhyme should be "natural" is not only desirable in and of itself, but also is required by an argument that depends on the craft and difficulty of writing it. Dryden explains that one must not let one's style pander to the rhyme, "as no man would in

16. "Essay on Poetry," in *Critical Essays of the Seventeenth Century*, ed. Joel E. Spingarn, 3 vols. (Oxford, 1908), II, 291–292. Hereafter, these volumes will be cited as "Spingarn."

ordinary speaking: but when 'tis so judiciously ordered, that the first word in the verse seems to beget the second, and that the next, till that becomes the last word in the line, which in the negligence of prose would be so, it must then be granted, rhyme has all the advantages of prose, besides its own" (Ker, I, 7).

Finally, he specifies the province as well as the potential virtues of the couplet: "Neither must the argument alone, but the characters and persons, be great and noble; otherwise, (as Scaliger says of Claudian) the poet will be *ignobiliore materiâ depressus.*" Howard replied in the preface to *Four New Plays* (1665) that the theoretical question depends on the ideal of a dramatic imitation, which to him included the feeling of spontaneity ("the present effect of accidents not thought of"); rhyme, Howard said, violated that feeling. His arguments, which Dryden gracefully put forth as Crites' in "The Essay of Dramatick Poesie" (1665), were answered by Neander (representing Dryden's position), in part by expanding points from the preface to *The Rival Ladies,* and in part—more significantly—by exploring the possibilities of decorum. Neander's reasoning here is striking and ingenious:

> It has been formerly urged by you, and confessed by me, that since no man spoke any kind of verse *extempore,* that which was nearest Nature was to be preferred. I answer you, therefore, by distinguishing betwixt what is nearest to the nature of Comedy, which is the imitation of common persons and ordinary speaking, and what is nearest the nature of a serious play: this last is indeed the representation of Nature, but 'tis Nature wrought up to an higher pitch. The plot, the characters, the wit, the passions, the descriptions, are all exalted above the level of common converse, as high as the imagination of the poet can carry them, with proportion to verisimility. Tragedy, we know, is wont to image to us the minds and fortunes of noble persons, and to portray these exactly; heroic rhyme is nearest Nature, as being the noblest kind of modern verse.   (Ker, I, 100–101)

Dryden tries to rebut Howard, that is, not by dealing with specific arguments, but by rejecting Howard's definition of the genre, by rejecting the central axiom from which the decorous propositions are deduced. Howard thinks of "tragedy" in terms of the object imitated as it is simply seen; Dryden, in terms of the means of imitation and of other noble or elevated literary forms.[17] Unfortunately, this sort of rebuttal left both men talking at cross-purposes, always an annoying experience, and when the same criticisms were rehashed, the controversy became less polite. Howard, in the preface to *The Duke of Lerma*, retired into languorous pomposity, while Dryden replied with the grinding sarcasm of his "Defence" (Ker, I, 110–133).

The charm of Dryden's prose, intelligence, and manner has led more recent critics to follow him in dismissing Howard as a simpleton unable to comprehend the force of his better's arguments until overwhelmed by them. Surely such a judgment is in error.[18] The force of Dryden's arguments presses out from a

17. Before Crites even broaches his argument, it has been negated by the whole previous discussion. Behind the humility and impartiality of the enterprise, in other words, Dryden has brought all four men to make the unstated assumption that drama involves above all its own mode of imitation, that all dramatic criticism properly converges on matters of technique. So much has been made of Dryden's objectivity that his elaborate rhetoric, by which one is brought to think of plays specifically in generic terms, has been overlooked. The *Essay* is as impartial as the *Meno*, Lucian's *Hermotimus,* or *The Hind and the Panther.*

18. It is an error given color by the indifference Sir Robert shows toward decorum in flaunting his whimsy in the use of rhyme (Spingarn, II, 107). But he was quite conscious, as would any educated man of the time have been, of decorum—the whole usefulness of the concept in discussing seventeenth-century criticism rests upon its having been everyone's overt literary presupposition—and his point, for example, that rhyme could not cope with simple directions such as "Shut the door" (Spingarn, II, 108) proves that he did think in terms of decorum. One may well suggest that his stated refusal to write by principle has more ostentatious negligence and malice in it than critical weight; in other words, that it is a reaction to the confident and (genteelly) dogmatic Dryden. Whatever his reasons were, in his arguments he proceeds from the nature of drama and develops his objections to rhyme on decorous grounds.

way of looking at the serious play which he himself later rejected; and if Howard felt compelled to yield to superior acidity
in 1668, he had the pleasure, in time, of redeeming his chagrin.
By 1678 he found himself the acknowledged victor. Since both
antagonists had reasoned from decorum, it was possible for Dryden to shift ground gracefully, if with a faint bitterness, without
renouncing principles as well as practice. With the publication
of *Aureng-Zebe*, the "Sisyphus of the Stage," as he now dubbed
himself, abandoned "his long-loved Mistress, Rhyme"; abandoned her, despite his epilogue's rather weary Parthian defense
of her honesty, for reasons which would have appealed to Howard: "Passion's too fierce to be in fetters bound, / And nature
flies him like enchanted ground." From this reference one cannot
tell whether the very nature of rhyme or the associations of
nobility it carried were responsible for Dryden's prosodic claus-
trophobia. The preface to *Troilus and Cressida* (1679) makes it
clear, however, that he has come to accept a theoretical position
closer to Howard's. For example, he bans "a perfect character of
virtue, [for] it never was in Nature, and therefore there can be
no imitation of it"; and says that "there is yet another obstacle [to
moving the passions] to be removed, which is pointed wit, and
sentences affected out of season; these are nothing of kin to the
violence of passion: no man is at leisure to make sentences and
similes, when his soul is in an agony. I the rather name this fault,
that it may serve to mind me of my former errors; neither will I
spare myself . . ." (Ker I, 210, 223). Dryden's attitude here
coincides with that which rejected rhyme as stiffly unnatural,
which stressed the verisimilitude of every moment and used the
universal, man, rather than the specific, hero. If the sheer bulk of
contemporary criticism on the use of rhyme is indicative of the
prevailing views, this revised position of Dryden's agreed with
the consensus.

A large number of criticisms concentrate on the unnaturalness
of rhyme; and by extension, if rhyme is defended through an
appeal to decorum, on the unnaturalness of the heroic play. Most

conservative are critics like Edward Phillips, who declares in the
preface to his *Theatrum Poetarum* (1675) that

> [As] for the Verse, if it must needs be Rime, I am clearly of
> opinion that way of Versifying, which bears the name of
> *Pindaric,* and which hath no necessity of being divided into
> *Strophs* or *Stanzas,* would be much more suitable for *Trag-
> edy* then the continued *Rhapsodie* of Riming Couplets,
> which whoever shall mark it well will find it appear too stiff
> and of too much constraint for the liberty of conversation
> and the interlocution of several Persons. (Spingarn, II, 270)

John Wright, the translator of Seneca's *Thyestes* (1674), provides only one instance of the broadened attack. In the prefatory
material (A8), he advises the reader that Seneca does not provide plot, love and honor, or "Bawd'ry A-la-mode"; however, he
goes on, the reader will find such devices of the current drama as
"High Lines, and Rime enough . . . , / And Sentences most
desperately Grave, / Dull Sence, and sometimes Huffs that Nature brave." The grouping casts contempt on all the appurte-
nances of heroic decorum.

Both sense and nature were offended by the rant—Wright's
"Huffs that Nature brave." "The Muse ran Mad," wrote Gran-
ville, in lines that are atypical only in their attempt to exculpate
Dryden:

> Our King return'd, and banisht Peace restor'd,
> The Muse ran Mad to see her exil'd Lord:
> On the crackt Stage the Bedlam Heroes roar'd,
> And scarce cou'd speak one reasonable word.
> *Dryden* himself, to please a frantick Age,
> Was forc'd to let his judgment stoop to Rage; . . .
> Deem then the Peoples, not the Writer's Sin,
> *Almanzor's* Rage, and Rants of *Maximin;* . . .
>   (Spingarn, III, 294)

Dryden himself reprehended extravagance in the dedication to
The Spanish Fryar (1681), in which he also defines "fustian" as

"thoughts and words ill-sorted, and without the least relation to each other" (Ker, I, 247). This is precisely the charge made against rhyme's required syntax and lexicon. Fustian— nonsense—demanded the tumidity of rant to make it theatrically effective; heroic energy, stifled by necessary rhyme, needed rant to make itself clearly visible; and the verse, bringing the requisite high style to the matter, thus pushed itself into extravagance. Further, such verse encouraged, by its own rhetorical and musical nature, a rhetorical and musical (i.e., an unnatural, "senseless") delivery by the actors. Again, in yet another way, one can see here the integrity of rhyme and theme (and, by extension, spectacle) in the heroic play. Attacks on the "high Rant, of Thundring, Rhiming Verse" implicated the whole type, with the possible exception of Boyle's plays.[19] And the same habit of mind

19. For the style of acting, see Alan Downer, "Nature to Advantage Dress'd," *PMLA*, LVIII (1943), 1002–1037, and John Harold Wilson, "Rant, Cant, and Tone on the Restoration Stage," *Studies in Philology*, LII (1955), 592–598. The rant was not the only histrionic freak of the heroic play; another was the lover's whine. See David S. Berkeley, "The Art of 'Whining' Love," *SP*, LII (1955), 478–496. Berkeley traces the extravagances of heroic lovers to the romance, and arrives at a syndrome of behavior, attitudes of mind expressed through attitudes of body. This amorous pattern, although it came somewhat later than did rant, complemented the bold honor of the heroic hero; or, as Lyrick says in Farquhar's *Love and a Bottle* (1699): "The Hero in Tragedy, is either a whining cringing Fool, that's always a stabbing himself, or a ranting, hectoring Bully, that's for killing every-body else."—*The Complete Works of George Farquhar*, ed. Charles Stonehill, 2 vols. (London, 1930), I, 51.

For other objections to rant, see Peter Belon, *The Mock-Duellist* (1675), who promises in his prologue to use only the "little Huff" rather than "Lines of Wonder" "That pose your Intellect, and th'Authors too." ". . . his accoast is gentle Nature's voice." In the epilogue to his *The Devil of a Wife* (1686), Thomas Jevon asks (H4ʳ):

> If you'l your thundering indignation vent,
> Let it on lofty bumbast all be spent.
> Applauded nonsense where sad lovers pine,
> And Hero's rant and fight and cry and whine;
> And the old buskins empty swelling strains,
> That cracks the Player's lungs and Poet's brains.

that was averse to rant was averse to all those other characteristics of the heroic play harmonious with and dependent on rant.

All the threads in this web of displeasure appear in such dismissals as Tom Brown's "The Play-House" from *Amusements Serious and Comical* (1700). Brown being what he was, one suspects that he felt compelled to be entertainingly satirical rather than to scourge the theatre. But he runs through arguments of those who did scourge the theatre, scornfully glancing at "Huffing *Dryden*" and at the unnaturalness of acting, of heroic heroes, and of rhyme. The "Collars of *Ay's* and *Eeke's*," if the comparison between "their Rhimes" and "Hopkins and Sternhold" is thorough, may refer to strained diction, padded lines, or both:

> The People [on stage] are all somewhat *Whimsical*, and Giddy-Brain'd: When they Speak, they Sing, when they Walk, they Dance . . . What are all their New Plays but Damn'd Insipid Dull *Farces*, confounded Toothless *Satyr*, or Plaguy *Rhiming* Plays, with Scurvy Heroes, worse than the Knight of the Sun, or *Amadis de Gaul* . . . and there's as much difference between their Rhimes, and Solid Verse, as between the Royal Psalmist, and *Hopkins* and *Sternhold*, with their Collars of *Ay's* and *Eeke's* about them.[20]

Buckingham's great *Rehearsal* (1672) undoubtedly represents the most devastating assault on the heroic play, including its

20. Pp. 51, 52. The hidden allusion to Don Quixote in mentioning the Knight of the Sun and Amadis de Gaul further amplifies and clarifies Brown's attitude in this scornful scoop of typical criticisms, criticisms that one finds continually reiterated by the enemies of rhyme. In fact, so typical is it that it is merely an adaptation of statements by Snarl in Thomas Shadwell's *The Virtuoso*. And here we have been led fortuitously to the richest fund of gall about rhyme, which Shadwell abused for some twenty years: see the preface and prologue to *The Sullen Lovers* (1668), the epilogue of *The Miser* (1672), the preface to *Psyche* (1675), the epilogue of *The Virtuoso* (1676), the opening scene of *Timon of Athens* (1678), and both the prologue and epilogue (by now superfetation) to *The Squire of Alsatia* (1688). Shadwell's comments are so thorough that they can serve as an empirical test of the sufficiency of the categories set up in this chapter.

rhyme. *The Rehearsal* not only seems to have made contempt for heroics fashionable—most of the criticisms came in the mid-1670's, a decade after the initial rhymed plays—but also to have precluded, by its success, further full-length burlesque. Despite its pointed brilliance *The Rehearsal* is neither obscure nor subtle, and since it has been admirably dissected elsewhere[21] I will pass it respectfully by. Many of the devices employed by Buckingham come up again in Thomas Duffett's farce, *The Empress of Morocco* (1674). This play, Drury Lane's counter to the *succès fou* that Settle's *Empress* had enjoyed with the Duke's Men, states its moral in its regular epilogue (following the comic epilogue spoken by witches "after the mode of *Macbeth*"):

> Farce and Heroick tale use but one fashion,
> Love and affection Layes the first foundation
> Then Gyant noyse and show set cheating Glass on.[22]   (H)

The direct target is Settle, but all heroic plays are so similar in technique (again, almost of necessity) that Duffett, like Buckingham's Drawcansir, "comes in, and kills 'em all on both sides." He parodies heroic theme—

> *Moren[a]*. I will do both—I can do neither.
> Revenge says go, honor does no say,
> Truly I do not know what to say   (D4^v)

—and heroic acting, as when Muly Labas spreads his arms, then thumps his breast, then weeps (E3^v). And of course, Duffett

21. Dane F. Smith, *Plays about the Theatre in England 1671–1737* (New York, 1936), pp. 9–37.

22. The reference to farce is interesting. Ravenscroft's prologue to *The Careless Lovers* (1673) makes the same charge; and, given the feeling that heroics were unnatural, that charge is perfectly intelligible. Dryden outlines the characteristics of farce in the preface to *The Mock Astrologer* (1671): farce consists of "forced humours, and unnatural events"; it "entertains us with what is monstrous and chimerical"; and it "works . . . on the fancy only" (Ker, I, 136). Dryden's "farce" approximates Ravenscroft's and Duffett's and Buckingham's "heroic play" with satisfying precision. Their objection to the one is his to the other, transversed.

mocks the use of rhyme. He exploits the absurdities of inversion, for example, Muly Labas' opening lines, "O *Morena* I am took napping / And must lay my head thy blew Lap in"; and forced rhyme—the Queen Mother's "But you may spare him tho' *Morena* / You know well enough what I mean a" (C2ʳ). Fanciful imagery, suitably lowered in tone (just as the poetic line is lopped a foot) produces Hudibrastic results, e.g., Hamet Alhaz'

> To day as I the wheat-Field stood in
> The sky was alter'd on a suddain,
> And look'd as thick as hasty pudding.   (D)

The lofty stations and foreign lands of the heroic play are mocked by transposition to menial and familiar settings, as with Buckingham's kings of Brentford. Thus Muly Labas is a corn-cutter, Muly Hamet a drayman, Mariamne a *"Scinder-Wench,"* and so on. As negative arguments for more exact mimesis, both *The Rehearsal* and Duffett's *Empress* are Butlerian, and therefore differentiated in technique from a mock-heroic like *Mac Flecknoe:* the standards of nature represented by Brentford and London are, as those in Dryden's London are not, themselves normative. In other words, we have a kind of parallel to the Dryden-Howard debate, with Dryden's norms generic, Buckingham's and Butler's referable to "real life."

It is at least improbable that such criticisms and Butlerian burlesques as I have been describing killed the heroic play through their critical force. One can both mock and enjoy the same work, even if the work demands being taken seriously; and at least some of the heroic plays, certainly when measured by their successors in favor, have enough aesthetic merit to withstand attack. I would suggest that the attacks were rather a device, an enabling clause by which the public discarded what it no longer wanted, what it no longer needed.

Here the public's motives remain problematical, although one may reject various possibilities. The heroic play did not go out of style because it was silly: even if it were silly, prolonged exposure to it should have dulled that recognition. Nor can neo-classic severity (see note 13 above) have acted quite so rapidly as it would have had to, to make heroic ornament offensive. Again, Shakespeare and Fletcher may have supplied the norms by which the approved critics judged, but unless one is to assume that tears have inherent delights over wonder, Shakespeare and Fletcher did not create a change in taste through their mere presence. History of ideas and study of repertory help one understand the forms which developed from the decaying fabric of heroics, but they cannot provide an adequate diagnosis of the patient's fatal malady. And yet heroics did die, before the displeasure of audiences who "increasingly demanded illusion, not artifice," whose needs insured that "the balance between engagement and detachment [in the heroic play] gave way increasingly to an emphasis upon engagement alone."[23]

Scholars have traditionally held that this dramatic change reflected a change in the composition, as well as the taste, of audiences. I think such a sociological explanation highly improbable. First of all, there is no evidence to support the theory of a radical change in the audience between 1670, when heroic plays were the most energetic and novel part of the repertory, and 1680, when most of them were "exploded" relics. Secondly, there is only the most dubious evidence to suggest that the Restoration audience changed appreciably before the reign of William and Mary. Pepys complained about citizens in the playhouse as early as 1662, and fretted over the "mean people" in the pit in 1668, when heroics were at their height.[24] If one is to believe Dennis,

23. Arthur C. Kirsch, *Dryden's Heroic Drama* (Princeton, 1965), pp. 33, 153. Kirsch's discussion of the whole matter of Dryden's rhyme, pp. 22–33 and 126–127, is cogent and highly intelligent. Also see the fourth chapter, "Rhyme and the Language of Tragedy" (pp. 93–122) in Sarup Singh, *The Theory of Drama in the Restoration Period* (Calcutta, 1963).

24. Quoted in *The London Stage, 1660–1800*, Part I, ed. William Van Lennep, with a critical introduction by Emmett L. Avery and Arthur H. Scouten (Carbondale, Ill., 1965), pp. cxlv–cxlvi. The notion of an elite audience in the early Restoration is also challenged by the facts presented in Emmett L. Avery, "The Restoration Audience," *PQ*, XLV (1966), 54–61.

and the implications of his statements, the less well educated appreciated the heroic play, while the men of taste deplored it. After linking Buckingham with a group of "extraordinary men at Court" who acted as censors of the public taste, he goes on to a specific example: "When The Town too lightly gave their ap[p]lause, to Half a Dozen Romantick, Ryming, whining Blustring Tragedies, allurd by their novelty and by their glare, then Villers Duke of Buckingham writt the *Rehearsall*, which in a little Time opend their eyes, and taught them to Despise what before They rashly admired."[25] He dates the changes in the audience from the Bloodless Revolution, by which time pathetic tragedy had been long established. Even after that, scant evidence exists to suggest any gross infiltration of the theatres by a demanding middle class in the seventeenth century. "Cibber, in the first years of the eighteenth century, accounting for the reverses of Betterton's company acting in Lincoln's Inn Fields [i.e., after 1695] mentions the theater's 'too distant Situation,' meaning, apparently, from the residences of the gentry, for the other theater then operating was Drury Lane."[26]

A further suggestion, that the numbers of women in the playhouse were increasing and influencing the drama, depends on circular reasoning from prologues and epilogues. No one can deny that much pathetic tragedy was directed to them, to the "matchless charms" (Prologue, *The Generous Conquerour*) of "Those tender Judges of Heroick Love" (Prologue, *Heroick Love*), those "Sov'reigns of Love, and Oracles of Wit" in their high-priced "bright Circle." But no one knows what the cause-and-effect relationship between their presence and pathetic tragedy may have been. Furthermore, it is by no means clear that women preferred pathetic tragedy to heroic plays; women had reveled in Caroline court drama and French romances, both of which share many romantic elements with the heroic play. Nor

25. *Critical Works of John Dennis*, II, 277.
26. John Loftis, *Comedy and Society from Congreve to Fielding* (Stanford, 1959), p. 14.

is it clear that female influence was great at a time when the brutal beauties of Wycherley and *The Man of Mode* were first enjoyed. In short, I should agree with John Lough when he writes, dealing with the growing dominance of love themes in seventeenth-century French tragedy, that the "contemporary tendency to put most, if not all, of the blame for this state of affairs on to women is not altogether convincing . . . [It is an] obvious fact that the majority of male spectators seem to have shared their taste for love themes in drama . . ."[27]

The speed of the change means that we must seek the explanation within the nature of the heroic play itself, not in the audience or the playwrights. We will find it in what one might call "formal exhaustion." The heroic hero serves as a pattern, an embodiment of the will and capability to achieve *gloire* and pure love. *Gloire* and love are paradoxical, in that they refer both to an external and objective set of public values, thus forcing the plays to exemplify them in highly generalized heroes, and to the self-aggrandizing ego of the hero, thus leading the plays to assert a radical individualism. Unlike Christian allegory and social epic, which justify their generalizing of character in the name of spiritual and social breadth, the heroic play glorified the individual too much to deal deeply with serious moral problems; unlike the later novel, its generalization barred it from dealing deeply with human psychology. When its situations and dramatis personae grew trite, it could turn to no remedy but that of sensationalism and ornament. Its own logic drove it inescapably in one direction; and through its developing immense efficiency at doing only one thing, it made itself a victim of technological

27. John Lough, *Paris Theatre Audiences in the Seventeenth & Eighteenth Centuries* (London, 1957), p. 158. The change in English tragedy closely parallels that in French tragedy, where Cornélian *gloire* ceded to the sufferings of the great in Racine and the "recherche obstinée et exclusive du pathétique" in Quinault. (Antoine Adam, *Histoire de la littérature française au XVII*[e] *siècle,* IV [Paris, 1958], 247.) The critic of English or of French literature might do well to frame his hypotheses about his own field of interest in the light of its analogue.

unemployment. For the theatre of the 1670's was discovering that the "sentimental" play could do half the heroic play's job, in whipping up the emotions of the audience, and the newly magnificent opera could do the other half, in cramming the public with sound, spectacle, and splendor.[28] Both forms were more flexible than the heroic play, offering more chance for variety precisely because they were less committed to principles other than those of pleasing.

If this explanation is accurate, it makes clear why the public of the seventies were increasingly ready to make the kinds of objections to heroics that I have been documenting, objections based on the ideal of a "natural" drama. Just as the Rapins and the Drydens were accommodating Aristotle to their own desires, so the critics of the heroic play used the catchwords of "imitation of nature" and "reason" to support a kind of drama that refused to divert attention from the characters by its ornamentation, that refused to distance the eager listener from the words and broken rhythms of pathos, that refused to let the egoism of greatness hamper the egoism of suffering. I do not mean at all to imply that the adversaries of heroic plays were engaged in a cabal to support sentimentality, but rather that their arguments prevailed only because the pathetic play and the opera could best the heroic play at its own game. It was to the advantage of those critics to leave the ideal of a "natural" drama undefined, as they did, and use it only as an agent of attack. To see what "natural" drama actually meant in the seventeenth century, how it made use of, or discarded, heroic machinery in calculations to please

28. The standard books on this subject are Edward J. Dent, *The Foundations of English Opera* (Cambridge, 1928), and Eric Walter White, *The Rise of English Opera* (New York, 1951). The comparison with French tragic development is complex, because Corneille found himself driven to more and more social themes, thus shutting himself off from the individual and psychological; Quinault and Racine to some extent filled in the gap that Corneille had left. Meanwhile, the opera was developing through ballet to the full-fledged spectacles of Lully, and partially took over the place of the Cornélian play.

the public, one must examine the plays themselves, as the last chapters of this study will do. In the meanwhile, one can appreciate that the significance of these attacks must be measured pragmatically. Criticisms of rhyme, and, by extension, of the heroic play, were heeded because they encouraged the excitement of softer passions, domestication, and concernment; protests that had less pragmatic value, such as those against lack of unity and sensationalism, were not heeded. Distaste for the aristocratic presumptions of the heroic play, such as one finds in the eighteenth century, could express itself only obliquely through the diminishing of the hero. However far the historian cares to call upon "good sense" or, foolishly, "spiritual stamina" as the source of the attacks on heroics, the nature of those attacks that seemed valid in their time depended on current theatrical possibilities and the prescription of a course for the drama to follow.

II

HISTORICAL DEVELOPMENT

3

THE REPERTORY
TRADITION

KNOWING THAT PEOPLE THOUGHT THE HEROIC PLAY "UNNAT-
ural," one is tempted to search the repertory for some "natural"
form of drama, of tragic drama, that could have provided them
with an alternative. Fortunately, calendars of performance dates
permit such an analysis of the plays staged by the King's and
Duke's Men.[1] For the first sixteen years of the Restoration, from
1660 through 1675, from 23 per cent to 24 per cent of performances were of tragedies. Well over half of these, 56 per cent to
57 per cent, represent performances of pre-war unrhymed tragedies, revivals of Fletcher, Shakespeare, Massinger, Suckling, *et
al.* Between 8 per cent and 9 per cent of the total, introduced or
revived Restoration plays. Only a little more than a third represent tragedies in rhyme. Even during their palmy years,
1664–1675, rhymed tragedies take up only 46 per cent to 48 per
cent of all performances of tragedies. It is true that these listings
have certain possible biases: since so much of the information
depends on courtly sources, more fashionable plays or playwrights might have been favored; or, again, new plays or produc-
tions might have attracted more attention than old. But these
biases hardly impugn—rather the opposite—what appears to be
the popularity of unrhymed tragedy. Even from this smattering
of dates, meager as it is, I think one would be justified in the
deduction that Restoration playgoers saw more unrhymed than
rhymed tragedy, and that the patterns of the unrhymed plays
might well have been in their minds when they objected to

1. See Avery, "A Tentative Calendar of Daily Theatrical Performances,"
and *The London Stage*, Part I. These percentages are inexact, because we do
not know enough to make them exact, but their significance is clear.

heroics. Those unrhymed plays, as my list indicates, can be broken down into two very unequal parts: one, the Restoration tragedies, comprises a small, although by no means insignificant part of the total, accounting for one play performed for every four rhymed plays; the other, Renaissance tragedies, dominates the field.

I shall discuss the unrhymed tragedies of the early Restoration in the next chapter, but neither the effect of those plays nor the development of the late heroic play can be considered without first surveying the influence of Fletcher and Shakespeare. Of these two, Fletcher was the more important, or at least the more nearly omnipresent. How his influence compared with that of such living playwrights as Dryden or Shadwell one cannot, of course, say with much certainty. But the statistical record is impressive: between one-sixth and one-seventh of the fare of the early Restoration theatregoer consisted of plays by Fletcher. Furthermore, the repertory of his plays was large. The list of plays allotted to Thomas Killigrew in January 1669 mentions some thirty-eight; Arthur Colby Sprague gives evidence for the actual production of thirty-three before the merging of the companies in 1682;[2] and we know of specific performance dates for twenty-seven before 1675. So extensive a familiarity with Fletcher's canon almost undoubtedly established his techniques, what Eugene Waith has called his "pattern," in playgoers' minds. With Shakespeare, a different situation prevailed. "Shakespeare's tragedies were popular in the Restoration. *Hamlet, Julius Caesar, Macbeth, King Lear,* and *Othello* have a long record of revivals. *Romeo and Juliet, Timon, Titus Andronicus* and *Troilus and Cressida* and the histories do not seem to have fared so well . . . But the comedies in general did not appeal to the Restoration . . ."[3] Here, presumably, attention would be more

2. Nicoll, *Restoration Drama*, pp. 353–354; Arthur Colby Sprague, *Beaumont and Fletcher on the Restoration Stage* (Cambridge, Mass., 1926).

3. John Harold Wilson, *The Influence of Beaumont and Fletcher on Restoration Drama* (Columbus, Ohio, 1928), p. 7.

likely to be focused on the particular play, on particular lines and scenes from a small number of frequently repeated tragedies; how frequently they must have been repeated can be estimated by the amount of critical attention paid them in the period. The kind of imitation that Shakespeare stimulated, then, might well stand in contradistinction to the kind of influence that Fletcher had.

During the mid-seventies, the living repertory of both Shakespeare and Fletcher appears to have altered, perhaps significantly so. Performance records are even sparser than usual between the conclusion of Pepys' diary and the early end-of-the-century newspaper advertisements, so that changes may be only apparent and conclusions are therefore tenuous; furthermore the merger of the companies in 1682 distorted the figures by cutting down on the number of plays put on. However, the available facts are these: if we divide Fletcher's early Restoration (1660–1675) repertory into two groups, those that survived into the period from 1675 to 1690 without suffering adaptation, and those that did not, we discover that only one of four tragedies was dropped, four of nine tragicomedies, but eleven of sixteen comedies. This significant change of balance also appears when we turn to the seven plays of Shakespeare's that carried over, unadapted, from the early Restoration to the period from 1675 to 1690. Only one of the seven—*The Merry Wives of Windsor*—was a comedy. The rest were either tragedies or histories that involved death and pathos, *Richard III* and *Henry VIII*. While such figures are hardly complete, their relationships do indicate increased interest in the serious plays of Fletcher and Shakespeare both. With this interest coincided the development of a new kind of tragedy, first in rhyme and then in blank verse, which concentrated on moving the passions.

I suggest that the sharpness of the change in tragedy owes a great deal to the presence, for the first time in the history of English drama, of a backlog of plays large enough to permit conscious borrowing, conscious imitation, conscious archaism.

When rhyme, encumbered and artful, was forced to yield its place to simple language, passion, and nature, the tragedians discovered that the existing repertory of Renaissance blank-verse tragedy could serve them as a warehouse of models. They wanted to do what they thought Shakespeare and Fletcher had done, and one only has to look at title pages and prefaces to see how extensive the Restoration itself admitted the imitation to be. *All for Love* is "Written in Imitation of *Shakespeare's* Stile"; Lee, in his dedication to his first completely unrhymed tragedy, *Mithridates, King of Pontus* (1678), says that he has endeavored "to mix Shakespeare with Fletcher; the thoughts of the former, for Majesty and true Roman Greatness, and the softness and passionate expressions of the latter, which makes up half the Beauties [of the play]"; Otway in 1679 "rifl'd . . . half a Play" from Shakespeare in his *Caius Marius*. One begins to find lines like "those Beauteous Tresses, / On thy Proud Fore-head, fixt with Horrour, stand, / Erected like the strutting Porcupine" (G3; Act V)—this example is from Settle's *Fatal Love* (1680).[4] Another index of interest is the number of outright adaptations. While Davenant's *Hamlet* and operatic *Macbeth* were the only tragedies or histories of Shakespeare's adapted between 1660 and 1675, except for the happy ending that Howard tacked to *Romeo and Juliet*, the next half-dozen years of the Restoration saw

4. In contrast, imitation of Shakespeare was unusual in heroic plays. *The Shakspere Allusion-Book,* for example, lists no accusations of plagiarism from Shakespeare leveled against heroic drama; and the indefatigable (and hostile) Langbaine can charge Dryden's rhymed plays with only one "plagiary" from all Elizabethan drama—the general claim that some part of *The Indian-Emperour* was first Fletcher's. Perhaps the earliest heroic dramatist to model much of his work on the Elizabethans was Lee, and his first play, *Nero,* opened in 1674. See *The Shakspere Allusion-Book* . . . , ed. J. J. Munro, 2 vols. (London and New York, 1909), II, *passim;* Langbaine, *English Dramatick Poets.* The difficulty with making any sort of confident statement on borrowings from the Elizabethans is that no scholar has labored through the heroic plays to make close annotations of earlier parallels. For whatever it may mean in light of such neglect, I know of no evidence of extensive borrowings of this sort.

Tate's *Richard II, King Lear,* and *Coriolanus,* Shadwell's *Timon,* Ravenscroft's *Titus Andronicus,* and Crowne's two adaptations from parts of *Henry VI,* as well as *Caius Marius.* Sprague's bibliography (in his book) of "Alterations and Adaptations" of the Beaumont and Fletcher plays shows a similar spurt of interest. Two such adaptations were printed between 1660 and 1675, thirteen between 1675 and 1700, neither of the former group and five of the latter being tragedies or tragicomedies.

Despite the growing popularity of certain Shakespearean tragedies, Fletcher remained more influential in the Restoration. The reason is, quite simply, that the Restoration read Shakespeare in Fletcher's terms of naturalness, pathos, and striking effects, rather than for the structural or symbolic or moral intelligence that modern critics admire. We must turn then to Fletcher's pattern, which we can discuss under five rubrics: (*a*) the plays are formal and rhetorical, but sustain the illusion of smooth easy conversation and a natural surface; (*b*) their plots are intricate, turning on improbable hypotheses; (*c*) the atmosphere is threatening; (*d*) consistency of character is sacrificed to situation and plot; (*e*) "an arrangement of dramatic moments" exploits emotional reaction and emotional diction so that the moments have individual meaning without contributing to an overall significance.[5]

Scholars have suggested that most of these rubrics also apply to the heroic play. The threatening atmosphere plainly is shared by Fletcher and the heroic playwrights. So are the intricacy of the plot, and the construction of plays through arranging "dramatic moments." Even here, I think, one must perceive this difference, that in Fletcher these moments essentially relate to the narrative, while in the heroic play they relate to the exhibi-

5. See Eugene Waith, *The Pattern of Tragicomedy in Beaumont and Fletcher* (New Haven, 1952). I have compressed in my discussion the eight heads under which Waith deals with the pattern on pp. 36–44 of his book. Also see Arthur Mizener, "The High Design of *A King and No King*," *MLN,* XXXVIII (1940), 133–154.

tion of character. Aspatia's lamentations and Amintor's bewilderment in *The Maid's Tragedy* are functions of the events of that play, while Almanzor's bewilderment over Almahide's seeming infidelity is a function of his character, to which the events of the play are subordinate. This distinction may seem tenuous, but nevertheless one should insist upon it. While Fletcher writes episodic narrative, heroic playwrights devote themselves far more to composing displays, dramatic booths to exhibit the heroic gesture and secure the admiration of the crowd.[6] The result is that the heroic hero seems oddly detached from the plot about him in the same way as Sherlock Holmes, say, is detached from the mystery on which he is intently working, because it exists primarily to display his deductive powers, his herohood. Even if Holmes should plunge over Reichenbach Falls—or Boyle's Mustapha submit to strangling at his father's command—one puts down the book with a final impression of the hero's spirit having triumphed rather than of the world's having victimized him. This is not a tragic effect, as tragedy is generally understood, whereas Fletcher's effects are tragic, in the Renaissance dramatic tradition of developing moral narrative. Fletcher may exploit this tradition cynically, but he remains within it as the heroic playwright does not. He provides characters whose essence is their ductility (point *d* above), drawing on a technique of characterization developed to show the fluctuations of the spirit within a stream of moral stimuli. The heroic hero owns his worth as a Calvinist his election, by fiat, and therefore cannot change but only reveal his fullness of merit.[7] Far from having his consistency

6. Here and later, I have used "heroic play" only for the full-blown heroic plays of Dryden and Settle, and those of Crowne, Pordage, and Durfey. Some of the characteristics of these plays are not shared by Cartwright and Boyle; but since I am interested in the effect of the heroic play on Restoration tragedy, I have deliberately simplified the term to apply to those plays closest in time to the tragedies that I discuss.

7. I am aware of the arguments of Scott Osborn ("Heroical Love in Dryden's Heroic Drama," *PMLA*, LXXIII [1958], 480–490), Jean Gagen ("Love and Honor in Dryden's Heroic Plays," *PMLA*, LXXVII [1962],

sacrificed to situation or plot, the hero then travels through the plot, which is almost always determined by forces external to him anyhow, in a sort of inner picaresque. The plot becomes the agent of change: Almanzor begins fiercely and ends in gentility because the series of situations in which Dryden has put him has elicited a series of altering but equally honorable responses. The heroic playwright, by ordering his situations carefully, can produce the dialectic effect of moral narrative without levying any moral tax on his Almanzors. The tragedians of the later Restoration tried to modify this technique, as we shall see.

As to the rhetoric of the plays, the Restoration found Fletcher's dialogue "natural," and that of the heroic play "unnatural," despite the direct line of descent. One cannot deny that the occasionally *précieux* tone and narcissistic self-consciousness of heroic drama comes from Fletcher. By the mid-1670's, however, there was so great a difference of degree that Restoration critics

---

208–220), and Eugene Waith (*The Herculean Hero in Marlowe, Shakespeare, and Dryden* [London, 1962]); these scholars claim that Dryden's heroes perfect themselves towards Renaissance ideals. Such arguments seem to me to result from a serious misunderstanding of heroic technique. One can adduce external evidence against them: for instance, if they were valid, one would expect to find moral movement in those plays of Dryden's which are more psychologically oriented, *Aureng-Zebe, All for Love, Troilus and Cressida, Don Sebastian,* and *Cleomenes.* Instead, with the dubious exception of Don Sebastian, Dryden's heroes are morally static in these plays. Furthermore, had Dryden's authority and enviable success lent glamor to the play of moral education, one might expect a good number of contemporaries and followers to have attempted similar plays. That other heroic playwrights did not write in the manner that Mr. Osborn and Miss Gagen claim for Dryden, undermines their argument. As to evidence from within the plays themselves, I would refer the reader to Kirsch's discussions in *Dryden's Heroic Drama.* One cannot deny that there are characters who reverse direction in the heroic play, but they do so mechanically. Professor C. D. Wood has suggested to me the image of that penny-arcade game in which one tries to shoot the electric eye in a moving clay bear; the bear, when shot, turns and moves in the direction opposite to that in which it had been going. Characters in heroic plays have this kind of electronic constancy and consistency, the shots that spin them being particularizations of love or honor, reason or passion. This procedure has nothing to do with moral crumbling or growing moral and ethical strength.

saw it as a difference of kind. The dramatic context, too, had changed. Fletcher's slick rhetorical dandyism was seen by Fletcher, presumably, against the background provided by Jonson and Marston and Shakespeare, but the Restoration saw it against the background of Dryden and Settle, or Durfey and Pordage—no wonder they only saw its naturalness. In imitating Fletcher, the playwrights of the later Restoration did produce formal and rhetorical verse, but largely, I would suppose, through their being legatees of the heroic play, since they strove to avoid the self-consciousness that accompanies formal rhetoric in Fletcher's work. As to the other points we have discussed, the new drama tried to alter the heroic norm towards the Fletcherian in every way. Each change followed or accompanied the demand for "nature" that we have seen in the criticisms of the heroic play.

I do not mean to suggest that the new drama actually turned out to be like Fletcher's. It did not, any more than Dryden's criticism turned out to be like Aristotle's. The significant differences are primarily emotional, and have their origins in the heroic play. Together with its "calculated balance between artifice and illusion, between detachment and engagement,"[8] the heroic play encouraged continual wish-projection, especially among men. Just as Wycherley's Horner lives in the midst of a masculine dream as old as the story of Gyges and as recent as the latest films, so does Almanzor. One's admiration for him is not only static—"admiration" in the old sense of wonder—but dynamic. Such immediate relationships between audience and hero, found in both Restoration comedy and the heroic play, did not really mark Fletcher's plays, with their concentration on plot. On the other hand, since the heroic play made plot subsidiary to character, or personality, it enabled such wish-projection to flourish. This habit of wish-projection remained useful to the late heroic playwrights when they began to realign the relationship

8. Kirsch, *Dryden's Heroic Drama*, p. 147.

between audience and character. Because the audience was drawn toward the hero and heroine almost independently of the plot, the late heroic play could have a far more shattering emotional effect than could the Fletcherian play. Here we may see the basis of Restoration "concernment." Its effect was to lead the late heroic play to greater and greater domesticity, despite the pull of Fletcher's technique toward increasing stylization. This is at least one of the reasons why Restoration tragedy, in its imitation of Fletcher's methods, evolved into so different a product.

4

THE RESTORATION
TRADITION

IN DEALING WITH THE DECLINE OF THE HEROIC PLAY, SCHOLARS have tended to overlook the importance of a living tradition of unrhymed tragedy. This is not surprising. The unrhymed tragedies written during the first fifteen years of the Restoration seem to be unconnected, to bob on the surface of the repertory at this point of time or that; they have neither novelty nor coherent direction. Critical attention and notoriety in the Restoration itself tended to focus on the heroic play, favored by the King and the French taste of the court, supported by the beauty and grandeur of scenery, the refined couplet, and the obvious interest of the important playwrights. As the attacks on rhyme show, the heroic play was something about which men were inclined to take strong stands. In contrast, the current of unrhymed tragedies was thin and quietly eccentric. There seems to be little temptation for the scholar to turn from Dryden, Settle, or even Boyle to study the work of Porter, Payne, Southland, Stapylton, and Sir Aston Cockain. Nevertheless, Porter, Payne, and the rest may very well be of great significance in theatrical history, because it was they who kept the Elizabethan tradition from becoming alien to the interests of Restoration authors. The criticism of Dryden, if nothing else, shows the keenness with which the Restoration felt its separation from pre-war England, the self-consciousness with which it regarded literary history. I suspect that within this intellectual atmosphere the imitation of the Elizabethans would have struck playwrights as perversely anachronistic, just as a modern musician's attempt to compose symphonies like Mozart's or Brahms' or a modern artist's to paint like Tintoretto would now strike his contemporaries. One admires but does not try to duplicate the past; the effect of unrhymed tragedy written before 1675 or so was to insure that the Renaissance tradition was not, absolutely, the Past. For this reason at least, it is worthwhile to look at these unrhymed tragedies, and briefly to trace their development.

Most of these plays follow either the revenge or the history tradition: they do not attempt, as the heroic play does, to combine personal and political concerns, private and public affairs. Perhaps the Elizabethanism, in which both revenge and history plays share, can be best indicated by looking closely at Porter's *The Villain* (1663), which Summers calls "a powerful drama, ably written and interesting throughout."[1] The tragedy turns on a pair of love rivalries. One develops between a general, Clairmont, and his officer, Brisac, over the hand of Charlotte, the daughter of the governor of a town in which Clairmont's regiment is quartered. This plot ends with a duel, eventually fatal to both men, and the madness of Charlotte, who has loved Brisac. The second and more important plot centers about Brisac's sister Belmont, secretly married to the officer Beaupres, and desired by the villainous subaltern Malignii. Malignii tries to destroy the trust between Beaupres and Belmont, and between Brisac and Beaupres. He also tries to rape Belmont himself. Finally, through conniving with a hot-headed dupe Boutefeu, he incites Beaupres to stab Belmont to death. The play ends with Malignii's capture and death by torture, and Beaupres' death from a broken heart.

The most immediately obvious "Elizabethan" quality of the plot is the direct borrowing from Shakespeare, particularly from *Othello*, which was the Shakespearean play most similar in structure to the Restoration pattern.[2] Malignii resembles Iago to the point of inheriting his tag of "honest" and his post of ancient, made into "subaltern" to fit the army instead of the navy. Despite

1. Montague Summers, *The Playhouse of Pepys* (reprinted New York, 1964), pp. 233–234.
2. This suggestion is also made by Roswell G. Ham, *Otway and Lee: Biography from a Baroque Age* (New Haven, 1931), p. 71.

the dull trudge of Porter's verse, Malignii's methods of calming anger at the suspicions he has raised remind one of Iago's:

> *Mal.* But you shall find how much unjust you are;
> Here, kill me, why don't you thrust? [*Opens his breast.*
> I'l die the Martyr unto Truth and Honor.
>   *Beau.* How's that, thou Devil?
>   *Mal.* Since that my friendship to your hopeful youth
> Has drawn me to this zealous folly,
> I ought to suffer for't;
> Hereafter you may live in ignorance: . . .   (F; Act II)

> *Iago.* . . . Take note, take note (O World)
> To be direct and honest, is not safe.
> I thank you for this profit, and from hence
> Ile love no Friend, sith Love breeds such offence.
>   *Oth.* Nay stay: thou should'st be honest.
>   *Iago.* I should be wise; for Honestie's a Foole,
> And looses that it workes for.   (III.iii.435–441)

And at the end of the play, detected in his machinations, Malignii refuses to give reasons for his treachery. Within this context, it is no wonder that Charlotte's song, in her melancholy madness, has the refrain, "Willow, Willow, Willow must I wear."

Furthermore, differences in specific content and genre divide Porter from the heroic playwrights. Malignii himself, as the villain of the title, exemplifies a Renaissance pattern. The Restoration villain, popularized by Settle in *The Empress of Morocco* (1673), represents a reworking of the traditional Machiavellian, and affords "at once the clearest indication of the continuity between the Elizabethan and Restoration drama and the most important gauge of important changes in technique."[3] The later Machiavellian desires power; the earlier glories in lust and the pleasures of guile. These "important changes in technique" separate Settle—who was fourteen when *The Villain* was staged

3. Louis Teeter, *Political Themes in Restoration Tragedy,* Unpublished Ph.D. Dissertation, Johns Hopkins University, 1936, chaps. iii; iv, pp. 153–154.

—not only from Shakespeare, but also, just as firmly, from Porter. Malignii is an Iago, not a Crimalhaz. The reasons for this are plain. Settle created his heroic villain to take over some of the dramatic functions of the "huffing" hero, and thus to free the hero from the sneering and swaggering that had become incumbent upon him as the heroic play developed.[4] But *The Villain* has no flights above a rather lofty domesticity, no heroic tradition behind it, no political plot at all. Ambition cannot have much force, so that the role of the hero remains relatively passive— Beaupres already has his Belmont—and the motive power behind the action, as in *Othello,* is the villain's. And there is still another consideration, apart from the differences in form that these differences in content prescribe: the heroic play, with its goal of inducing admiration, was unable to let a Machiavellian dominate the action. The Machiavellian works too privately and unheroically. The heroic analogue had to be something like *Tyrannick Love,* in which the villain is publicly available, as it were, for the world to respond to; here Dryden's (Neander's) comparison of the heroic figure to a huge statue, self-contained and self-regarding, seems especially well chosen. Porter, on the other hand, does not aim at admiration. The style and scope of his tragedy remain too low.

The dominance of Malignii is further stressed by the sharing of the hero's role, divided between Brisac and Beaupres, and the relative failure of both these men—one dies in mid-play, and the other murders his innocent wife. In line with Porter's lack of interest in evoking admiration, these heroes have no extravagant rant of the sort that is the castemark of the high heroic play. The only huffing speech in *The Villain,* one of Clairmont's (H3ʳ), places him in his dramatic position as rival to Brisac and as

4. Teeter, p. 106, speaking specifically of *Aureng-Zebe,* writes that the Machiavellian, "with his boasts and rants and his contemptuous treatment of the emperor, has taken over, in part, the function of the rebellious hero and permitted the dramatist to develop the character of the hero along lines more consistent with decorum and kingly dignity."

antithetical parallel to Malignii; it brings him no admiration. Again, Porter holds to Elizabethan practice. There is rant in Elizabethan plays, of course, but its function is not that of rant in heroic drama. The Elizabethan play *characterizes* through its use of rant, while the heroic play, working within a different scheme of expectation, uses rant to *categorize*. Clairmont, Cethegus in *Catiline*, Bussy D'Ambois, or for that matter Hotspur—each makes clear through his rant what sort of individual he is; but heroic rant specifies the established theatrical context within which the character belongs. While exaggerated rhetoric in Renaissance plays indicates that the speaker is unbalanced, almost no exaggeration is too great for the heroic hero whose speech is an index of stature and not psychology: one can even accept the heavy brilliance of Dryden's Maximin, or of Durfey's Moaron who cries out, "I'l rip my breast, and drown thee with my blood." Unlike Maximin and Moaron, Clairmont is not the principal man of the play in which he appears.

Finally, *The Villain* not only operates at a less grandiose level of style than does the heroic play, but it also incorporates a much wider range of styles. It mingles tragic and comic elements as does no rhymed tragedy from Cartwright's in 1661 to Charles Hopkins' at the end of the century.[5] In the Elizabethan manner, Porter prefers breadth of social scope to consistency of tone, and he devotes considerable time to the antics of the whoremaster officers in an inn run by a low innkeeper, his buffoonish son Colignii, and his sluttish daughters. Colignii, as Cibber points out in praising Anthony Leigh's portrayal, can be very funny indeed: "Characters that would make the Reader yawn in the Closet, have, by the strength of his [Leigh's] Action, been lifted into the lowdest Laughter on the Stage. Of this kind was the Scrivener's great boobily Son in the *Villain*."[6] The disparity

5. On the theoretical principles of decorum, Kirsch and Singh are useful, as is C. V. Deane, *Dramatic Theory and the Rhymed Heroic Play* (London, 1931).

6. Cibber, *Apology*, I, 146.

between Colignii's idiotic behavior and his heroic name, taken from the great French admiral, sets up a sort of mock-heroic, and emphasizes these low scenes as a counterpoint to the scrupulous ideals of the main plots. In the heroic play, we come no closer to this typical Renaissance mode of construction than the use of a docile hero and heroine, like Ozmyn and Benzayda in *The Conquest of Granada,* to set off the principals, and then, of course, the effect of one plot on the other is quite different.

Some of the same characteristics that set *The Villain* within a Renaissance tradition recur in the Viscount Falkland's *The Mariage Night* (1664), which is very much like *The Villain* in style and timbre; here the model is not Shakespeare but the Jacobean gloom of Marston or Webster.[7] A scheming Duke forces a malcontent henchman into vengeance, as with Webster's Ferdinand and Bosola, while the affections of the henchman, Dessandro, allegorically imitate his increasing subjection by turning from his betrothed Cleara to the Duke's secret mistress, Claudilla. This moral movement recalls Vendice (*The Revenger's Tragedy*) or Antonio (*Antonio and Mellida,* Part II), the man crippled (*claudicatus*) by passion from the noble honor (*cleos*) that itself brought the passion into being. The allegorical treatment of the names, too, reminds one of *The Revenger's Tragedy* or *The Broken Heart,* or of Malignii and Boutefeu in *The Villain,* rather than of the historical or deliberately exotic names of heroic drama. And the emphasis on a psychological moral life harks back to the Renaissance rather than the Restoration, surely rather than the Restoration heroic play. Admittedly, heroic characters are frequently conceived in moral, almost allegorical, terms, or categories; the plays themselves may be designed to

7. Fredson Bowers discusses it in *Elizabethan Revenge Tragedy* (Princeton, 1940), pp. 252–258; he says that it was "written at some indeterminate date after 1642," but presumably before 1660. Since Henry Cary (not, as Bowers has it, George), the Viscount, was born in 1634, the play can hardly predate the 1650's. It was performed in 1667, when Pepys saw it (March 21), presumably in a more coherent version than that extant.

accord with providential or poetic justice; but the subtleties of internal alteration, the slow spoiling of heart, remain foreign to the Restoration playwright. The pre-war dramatists, however, along with Falkland or Porter, dwell on moral change: Middleton's Beatrice-Joanna, Chapman's Bussy, Hemmings' Castrato/Crotilda, as well as Vendice and Antonio, are morally destroyed by their commendable motives. If further clarification is needed, a mental comparison between the moral allegory in either of the first two books of *The Faerie Queene* and that in, say, *Pilgrim's Progress* or *The Holy War* (in which characters do deteriorate morally, but in a different way) should illustrate this distinction.

From *The Villain* and *The Mariage Night*, which were roughly contemporary with Boyle's *The Generall* (October, 1662) and *The Indian-Queen* (January, 1663), through the twelve years' vogue of the heroic play, the descendents of the Elizabethan revenge play maintained a trickle of life. As late as 1672, Dorset Garden saw Nevil Payne's capable tragedy *The Fatal Jealousie,* appearing well after the work of Boyle, Dryden, Settle, and Crowne had become standard in the repertory. All the points made about *The Villain* apply to *The Fatal Jealousie.* The entire plot, as the blank verse would demand, lies lower than is ever the case with heroic tragedy. No political theme lifts *The Fatal Jealousie* to a public level, even so factitious a public level as characterizes the heroic play. As a result, the Machiavellian Jasper, played by the famous Malignii, Sandford, fits in the Renaissance mold. He does dote on revenge, upon the "Family, who Rise upon the Ruines of our House" (B3; Act I), but this motive is stressed no more than are Iago's potpourri of excuses or Malignii's strange love for Belmont. We are again reminded that the vice and revenge traditions, through which the Porter and the Payne plays descend, stress the process of villainy and of moral corruption far more than the motives; that is why heroes can fall when their conscious motives are quite honorable. In the heroic play, on the contrary, villains almost always pay obeisance to the heroic ideals: they are motivated by a desire for some form of love or honor, and the characteristic pattern of the plays is one of rivalry, not of stark malice. Renaissance practice is so far from this that the Machiavellian character frequently is a person of no station or low station, a subordinate like Iago or Malignii or Dessandro, or an outcast like Kyd's Hieronymo, Chettle's Hoffman, and Payne's Jasper. Iago, Malignii, and Jasper link a lower and seamier life to the tragic plot; in both *The Villain* and *The Fatal Jealousie* that lower life is comic, and a great deal goes on that is outside the pale of high decorum. The comic Colignii in Porter, for instance, is paralleled by Payne's decaying but lecherous nurse, to whom Jasper prostitutes himself. This part gains emphasis by its having been written for James Nokes, "the greatest farceur of the whole period," in petticoats.[8]

As in *The Villain*, the function of the hero in *The Fatal Jealousie* is divided among a number of flawed men who are subject to Jasper's Machiavellianism. Again as in *The Villain*, Shakespeare's plays have been drawn upon heavily; in his edition of the play, Willard Thorp notes "at least fourteen" certain echoes of, or parallels to, Shakespearean texts, including *Othello* and *Hamlet*. Of these fourteen, he offers three examples of "unmistakable echoes," each of which is convincing as an evidence of Payne's having foraged in Shakespeare.[9] Not to belabor the point, then, *The Fatal Jealousie* resembles *The Villain* rather closely, and its production in 1672 indicates that the Restoration audience did not find the tradition that both plays represent anachronistic. That tradition, proved at least tenuously viable, could legitimately be drawn upon as the heroic play began radically to change.

The second of the genres to descend from pre-war drama, the

8. Leo Hughes, *A Century of English Farce* (Princeton, 1956), p. 36. For a general discussion of Nokes' abilities and typical roles, see Hughes, pp. 169–174.

9. Henry Nevil Payne, *The Fatal Jealousie* (1675), Augustan Reprint Society publication, Series 5, No. 2 (1948), p. 5.

historical tragedy, had no such constancy during the Restoration. To follow its course, I should like to look at two plays, John Wilson's *Andronicus Comnenius* (1664) and Edward Howard's *The Usurper* (1668), both of them stimulated by Cavalier reaction to the murder of King Charles and the rule of the Cromwells. Such topical material is by its very nature changeable, especially since Renaissance conventions for history were nowhere nearly so helpful in offering formal patterns as were those for the revenge play, or Cavalier drama, or humours comedy. The impulse toward stability of form inevitably moved the historical tragedy further from such topical propaganda as Dryden's *Amboyna* and closer to the stylization of politics characteristic of the heroic play.

Andronicus Comnenius uses the usurpation, bloody reign, and bloodier death of Andronicus I, Emperor of Constantinople, as a story relevant to Commonwealth England. Perhaps Andronicus' and Cromwell's deaths on approximately the same day in September (in 1185 and 1658, respectively) called attention to the comparison and clinched it symbolically; for whatever reason, three plays published in the early years of the Restoration, of which *Andronicus Comnenius* is the best, use the same story for the same purpose. One of the three plays, the anonymous *Andronicus: a Tragedy* (1661), justifies the seventeenth-century critic who wrote at both front and back of the British Museum copy, "Verry Badd." Its only distinction, other than its documentary importance and its strongly royalist verses on the martyr king, is that it may enjoy the only spondaic decasyllabic line in English drama: Lapardas, when his eyes are bored out, has the speech, "O, O, O, O, O, O, O, O, O, O." *The Unfortunate Usurper* (1663) is so nondescript as to be hardly worth discussing. *Andronicus Comnenius* represents a decided improvement over either, as one might expect from the author of *The Cheats;* and just as *The Cheats* and *The Projectors* imitate Jonson's comic style, *Sejanus* must have been the helpful model for *Andronicus Comnenius.* There are also passages in which Wilson steals from Shakespeare: when Andronicus woos Alexius' widow in Act IV, "the dramatic dialogue is abstracted, almost word for word, from Shakespeare's *Richard III*."[10] I do not know if Wilson hit upon these allusions merely as means of expressing Andronicus' wickedness or if the reader was meant to pick them up and amplify his literary response. It is certain that the allusiveness limits what Wilson does, for he addresses himself so strictly to the analysis of tyranny after the method of *Richard III* and *Sejanus* that the kind of private plot that would dominate a heroic play does not occur here. Even the appearance of Andronicus' virtuous son Manuel provides ethical contrast, not sentimental or even "humanizing" familial relationships. Shakespeare, Jonson, and Wilson give the moral of their respective historical fables the climactic position: Richmond's "Abate the edge of Traitors, Gracious Lord," and even more the bestiality of the mob at the end of *Sejanus* find their echo here in Constantinus' earnest moralizing about rebellion and usurpation, and his damning "The uncertain people, / Constant to nothing, but inconstancie" (M3ʳ).

If one looks more closely at the stylistic consequences of imitating the Elizabethans, one can see further differences between plays like Wilson's and the heroic drama. In these differences there are hints of some reasons for the continuing fascination of Renaissance techniques during the Restoration, stylistic reasons that supplement our discussion of the Fletcherian pattern. I am thinking specifically of Wilson's development of the rabble scene, which was to become a favorite device of politically-oriented tragedies after 1675. The lower level of generic decorum common to all the unrhymed plays of this period allows

10. M. C. Nahm, "John Wilson and his 'Some Few Plays'," *Review of English Studies*, XIV (1939), 153. A list of all borrowings from pre-war writers is provided by Karl Faber in *John Wilsons Dramen. Eine Quellenstudie* (Wiesbaden, 1904), pp. 42–49. Many of Faber's parallels are dubious, but there are certainly enough that are valid to show the strong influence of the earlier drama on Wilson.

Wilson to introduce the populace in all its boisterous stupidity
upon the stage. Ostensibly, the function of rabble scenes is to
extend the consequences of the main action into a larger social
group, not to parody the main action in the manner of subplots
in *The Villain* or *The Fatal Jealousie;* but the same stylistic
conditions gave leeway for low scenes in both cases, and the
immediate effect upon the audience must have been rather similar. In any event, scenes such as this from *Andronicus Comnenius* later proved stock fare:

> *Omnes.* Liberty—Liberty—Liberty: [*A Hollow.*
> 1 *Cit.* But hark you neighbours—We must have some
> Government.
> 2 *Cit.* Time enough to think of that hereafter;—Let's
> destroy this first.
> 3 *Cit.* What think you of Aristotocracy?
> 4 *Cit.* No, no, no—Oligasky for my money.
> 5 *Cit.* By your favour neighbour, I should think Democo-
> cracy.
> 6 *Cit.* And with your favour too; why not Anarchy?
> 2 *Cit.* Any thing, any thing but what we are:
> *Omnes.* Liberty—Liberty—Liberty—[*A Hollow.*
>
> (L2; Act V)

Not even the Toryism, or Loyalism, of the heroic playwrights
could bring them to include such scenes in the heroic play; if
rhymed tragedy had not been dying by the time of the Popish
Plot, surely the need to dwell on topical reference would have
killed it at that time.

One can make the same kind of observation about sexual
candor. The dry geometries of Boyle passed, as the heroic play
developed, into increasingly fervid expressions of passion, potentially salacious if not bawdy. But full sexual candor was hardly
heroic. The heroic playwright found himself cut off from the
natural development of his themes, and from the profitable sexu-
ality mined by Restoration comedy, while the unrhymed drama
offered the chance of frank dialogue. Not only in revenge plays

like *The Fatal Jealousie,* which concentrates on whoring and cuckolding, or Sir Aston Cockain's *Tragedy of Ovid* (1662), which is full of meaty sensualism, but also in the unrhymed history play, sex offers titillation. Wilson himself is restrained, but in *The Unfortunate Usurper,* for instance, the lustful Xene remarks philosophically:

> Were it not for this Knowledge [afforded by the senses],
> Our rarest delicacies would afford us
> No better relish then the poor Russet-Tenants
> Meaner Fare; then our *Caveare, Eringo* Roots,
> *Potatoes,* and *Chocolate,* and the rest
> Of the Train-bands of high dishes would be in vain
> Muster'd together to defend
> Our lusts from being mortify'd and kill'd,
> By frequent skirmishings in *Cupids* Camp;
> Then would our *Dildoes* be of no great use,
> Our Eunuchs, Marmosets, and young Pages
> Would do us little service. (C4; Act I)

One can hardly imagine Dryden's Nourmahal discussing self-priming with a dildo. In Boyle's tragedies, nearest the Andronicus plays in time and farthest from them in mode and style, a speech like this would be unthinkable. The artistic merits of such freedom are debatable, I suppose, but one can understand perfectly why playwrights turned with relief to a decorum that permitted freedom of language and reference, once the peculiar virtues of the heroic style had begun to tarnish.

However, before the history tradition could offer its special idiom to the heroic play for some sort of synthesis, it had to be reshaped. Dramatists could swallow the revenge tradition almost straight, because they were moving toward the same goals of pathos and sensuality that it expressed. The history play as Wilson wrote it was foreign to those goals, and playwrights had to maneuver it closer to the prevailing idiom. This is the process we find working in Edward Howard's *The Usurper* (1668). Although Edward Howard, like his brother Robert, protested the popularity of the rhymed play, he was no novice at dealing with heroic forms or ideals. After *The Usurper*, he was responsible for two heroic poems, *The British Princes* (1669) and *Caroloiades* (1689). One might expect *The Usurper* to be unrhymed but close to heroics, and so it is. Howard purports to be writing about the same usurpation as Wilson, but there is immense difference in their treatments of the theme. Wilson's allegory of Andronicus, despite the unjust (perhaps unintentional) contumely it casts on King Charles I, resembles the actual historical situation, while that of *The Usurper* wanders off into schematic fantasy. As Boas justly remarks, "Cleomenes and Hugo de Petra might pass for Monck and Hugh Peters; but a usurper who murdered his son, and an exiled king posing as a Moor, and marrying an African queen, were very far-fetched representations of Cromwell and Charles II."[11] "Cleomenes" presumably alludes to the general who freed Athens from the tyrannic family of Pisistratus; "Damocles," the name of the Cromwell in the play, must refer to the famous sword-fearing flatterer who lived a century later; while the protagonists, Cleander and Timandra, take their names from simple Greek compounds, "glorious man" and "woman of honor." In other words, there is no attempt at actual historical fact, or, given "Hugo de Petra," linguistic consistency. Correspondingly, the emphasis of the play is not on the political distress of a real or fictional Sicily, but upon the individual characters. Howard makes much of the love plots and the heroic, or at least grandiose, *sprezzatura* of Damocles: "There's the Delight, the mischief is my Luxury; / To Raise 'em high, then Crush 'em in their Swelling" (C; Act I). Cleander's language, too, shines in the high style, and he himself worships heroic values:

> . . . But were
> Our Persons singly arm'd, and we two plac'd

---

11. *The Change of Crownes, a Tragi-Comedy by the Honorable Edward Howard*, ed. Frederick S. Boas (London, 1949), p. 3.

Upon a Cliff, or some Star-kissing mountain:
All thy abused Legions round about us
Staring to see us fight for Love and Honour:
The Gods should not be weary to look down, . . .

(H3ᵛ; Act IV)

Perhaps even more important, one finds certain dramatic devices characteristic of the heroic play, such as a father-son love rivalry, intrusions of action unnecessary for the plot, and the manipulation of events through external forces (like the convenient revolution at the end).

The fullest synthesis of the history and heroic traditions comes in Nevil Payne's *The Siege of Constantinople* (1675), the first real wedding of blank verse and rhymed forms. This play, with *The Villain*, is perhaps the most significant unrhymed tragedy of the period, coming as it does at a time when the heroic play, through men like Lee and Otway, was reaching for what it could glean from blank-verse plays. *The Siege of Constantinople* enjoys a heroic plot: love strikes postures in the foreground while the background is filled with the images of political and martial struggle. Thus Payne can show the hero, Thomazo, demonstrating his valor in the first act by driving off two masked ruffians who have accosted his beloved and her companion; and in the second act, by driving off the attacking Turks almost singlehandedly. Thomazo's love is constant, intense (he goes mad when he thinks Irene is lost), and directed towards a worthy lady; his speech glitters with the proper heroic ornaments. In Act I he declaims: "All I seek, / Is bright unsully'd glory: I'de not be / Sole Monarch of the world by one base deed" (B2), and five acts later (L3ᵛ) can still maintain, despite his maddening intensity of amorous passion: "No, Brother, / *Thomazo's* Love and Fortune shall give way / When's Honour, or your safety is in question." Appropriately, his dreams are

   . . . made of sweet and pleasant walks,
By Crystal streams, set all with Bays and Mirtle;

> Or else in Fields, where every step I take,
> I meet a Love, or joyful Victory.   (B2ʳ; Act I)

Dreams, in the pre-Freudian clarity of the seventeenth century, indicated realities rather than frustrations; and the fortuitous death of the Emperor leads to the rewards of both love and honor.

Typically, the evil Chancellor offends against both: like villains in Joyner's *Roman Empress, The Usurper,* and a number of the heroic tragedies, but unlike those in most of the unrhymed plays, he is a lustful traitor. Thus Lorenzo recommends the brothel of "Mother *Somelies*" to the Chancellor: "You know she always fits you with fresh Girls" (Eʳ; Act II). At the end of that act, the Chancellor actually appears with prostitutes, and concludes with: "I cannot live an hour without a Woman; / Oh they're the useful'st Creatures . . ."(F). As to honor, an allegorical masque (D; Act I) tells what the action shows, that the difference between corrupt and heroic honor is that between "Ambition" and "Fame." The Chancellor thus can be put forth as an appropriate antagonist to Thomazo, who complains: "This Chancellour, like some unlucky Star, / Does interpose his Direful Influence / Through all my Happiness in Love or Honour" (E3; Act II). As usual, the hero is subject to the rule of another (here, the Emperor); as usual, there is love rivalry; as usual, the outcome of the play hangs not upon the hero's accomplishment but on some external force (here, the virtue of the Turks and the death of the Emperor). There are further signs of heroic influence, such as the imitation of the punishment scene in *The Empress of Morocco* (1673). This shocking scene, visually preserved in the last of the six engravings in Settle's text, shows naked corpses impaled. *The Siege of Constantinople,* produced sixteen months later at the same theatre, ends with *"a great Number of Dead and Dying men in several manners of Death's. The* Chancellor, Lorenzo, *and* Michael *Empal'd."* And as a

Machiavellian, the Chancellor follows the pattern established by Settle.

And yet, Payne does not abandon the techniques of such plays as his *Fatal Jealousie*. The scope of decorum is wider than is at all common in heroic drama, e.g., the episode in which the Chancellor's poisoned henchmen reel about *"doing mad things"* (F4; Act III). Bawdry even comes close to Irene in an ironic moment which both demonstrates and exposes her naïveté: the boy Kecko, itself a suggestive name, comes in singing a song in which young Adonis catches a bee; when Venus' eye drops a tear, he cries

> Oh! forgive me, I will bring
> A bigger and a longer Sting.
> Smiling, she cry'd, pretty Lad,
> When that time comes, I'le be glad.   (Gᵛ; Act III)

Irene responds to the song with: "I see there still is left some Innocence / To keep the World from sinking." Such inclusions permit a more flexible tone, and, as they mingle with the main plot, force the play towards greater realism.

In short, one may trace two streams of unrhymed tragedy from the Renaissance to 1675. One of them, the revenge tradition, changed very little because its ends were pretty much those to which the developing heroic play was beginning to move in the 1670's. Although there are no more than a few plays in this mode, their influence as a viable tradition must have been supported, not only by the Elizabethan repertory through which the theatre thrived, but also, I suspect, by the appetite for private intrigue that new comedies and tragicomedies excited. The second tradition, that of the history play, lay to the windward side of heroics. It offered useful patterns to the changing heroic play only by veering radically until it had become a simple alternative to heroics, doing most of the things that the heroic play did, but presenting in addition the advantages of great freedom in style and configuration of plot. The proponents of more "natural" drama must have welcomed new ways of writing tragedies which were not committed to loftiness and *grands amours,* and the playwrights welcomed a breadth of style that taxed their ingenuity less strictly. Eventually the welcome was to go sour, but in 1675 no one could know that.

5

THE LATE HEROIC
PLAY

THE HEAT OF CHANGE BEGAN TO GLOW PERCEPTIBLY THROUGH the late heroic play, the first efforts of Lee, Banks, Otway, and others. A greater stress on pathos was the most noticeable of its several effects. To some extent, of course, the heroic play had always made use of the pathetic, even in the hands of Dryden and Settle. Ozmyn and Benzayda in *The Conquest of Granada* represent a sweet domestic virtue, and thus are eligible for sentiments of pity. Abenamar's melting repentance for his past cruelty, for example, might serve as prototype for the sympathetic familial clusters that Dryden's successors so carefully designed to draw generous tears. Or, again, the young lovers in *The Empress of Morocco*, Muly Labas and Morena, open that play with a sustained lamentation, a bit of sentiment that the late Restoration was to employ to unfortunate excess. However, even the casual reader of those plays can see that such episodes are subordinate to the episodes of audacity, of heroic passion, of what Dryden called "excessive and overboyling courage." Neither formally nor emotionally can pathetic scenes be central in the full heroic play. They almost never involve the main characters—Ozmyn and Benzayda, for instance, merely fill out the context for Almanzor, giving it scope, contrast, and tone. This must be true, because no play can pursue awe and admiration at the same time that it disgraces hero and heroine with the indignity of public pity.

Pity implies superiority and parity: he who pities willingly resigns within his own mind his superiority of condition, and imaginatively lowers himself to the condition of the man he pities. It is no wonder that pity became the favorite short answer of the benevolists to the Hobbesians, for pity rebukes Hobbes on his own ground. It not only proves men capable of altruism and brotherly love, but also insists that the very conditions that Hobbes thought inevitably produced the comfort and laughter of egoism, were conditions that in fact led to a willingness to divest the mind of its established superiority. To elicit pity, then, as the Restoration perfectly well realized, the audience must be shown distress and also invited to make analogies to their own imaginary experience. Perhaps this last invitation comes less from a way of writing than from a way of seeing, but even if this is so, an audience must be initiated into a way of seeing by the play's establishing its images of our world, its own standards of *vraisemblance*. The heroic play, in the hands of authors from Dryden to Durfey, relishes *invraisemblance*. It deliberately molds itself around characters of vastly expanded autonomy, characters whose choices are true as their spirits are great, whose perfection tends to destroy their humanity and to crowd aside their world as anything but an adjunct to their grandeur. In thrusting the exceptional man into such prominence, the heroic play shows itself of Hobbes' time, and furthermore (as no one has pointed out) encourages the self-aggrandizing of the audience who exalt themselves to the importance of Almanzors. Pity is at most a gracious concession by the audience of a heroic play. Moreover, in the very crowding aside of the world, the playwright annihilates the preconditions of pathos, which must exploit situation—what happens to the characters rather than what they do. Passivity denies the essence of the heroic play.

Not even the serial construction of the heroic play can admit pathos, because all the scenes need to be held together by a consistency of style. In this regard, the heroic play and its hero typify the results of the Restoration habit of intellectual simplification, refinement, pursuit of things to their purity. As Mrs. John Evelyn wrote Ralph Bohun in 1671 about *The Conquest of Granada*: "Love is made so pure, and valour so nice, that one would imagine it designed for an Utopia rather than our stage. I do not quarrel with the poet, but admire one born in the decline of morality should be able to feign such exact virtue."[1] Without necessarily sharing in her admiration, we can recognize the justice of her appraisal.

For these reasons, perhaps for others as well, pathos cannot be central in heroic drama. Because the distinctions above are stated as absolutes, they admittedly distort facts toward extremes: the introduction of the pathetic was, like all historical processes, gradual, and one should not make too little of such stirrings as the Ozmyn and Benzayda episodes as the 1670's began. By and large, however, theory and facts jibe in this case, and the gathering force of antagonism that we have examined above indicates how few concessions the rhyming playwrights could or would make. When the heroic play entered its late period, practice did begin to swerve sharply from precept. The result is a freakish and unstable—because only momentarily justifiable—form, the denatured rhymed tragedy. The group includes *Aureng-Zebe* (produced 1675), Settle's *Ibrahim* (produced 1676), Lee's *The Tragedy of Nero* (produced 1674), *Sophonisba* (produced 1675), and *Gloriana* (produced 1676), Otway's *Alcibiades* (produced 1675) and *Don Carlos* (produced 1676), and Banks' *The Rival Kings* (produced 1677), among others. From the pattern established by these plays emerged the unrhymed tragedy of the late seventies and eighties.

Rochester's tart contempt for *Sophonisba*, in his "Allusion to Horace," is not very interesting for his calling Lee a "hot-brain'd *Fustian Fool*"—that opinion was common enough. But his annoyance that Hannibal should be made "a whining Amorous *Slave*" marks the old guard's impatience with the new drama of feeling. Most of the whining in fact was assigned not to Hannibal but to Massinissa, King of Numidia, a part so important that

1. John Evelyn, *Diary and Correspondence . . . to which is subjoined the private correspondence between King Charles I. and Sir Edward Nicholas, and between Sir Edward Hyde . . . and Sir Richard Browne*, ed. William Bray, 4 vols., (Bohn's Historical Library) (London, 1859), IV, 25.

Lee entrusted it to Charles Hart, who, ironically, had created Montezuma and Almanzor. Massinissa is discovered, in the second scene of the play, sitting with his nephew and his confidant in "a pleasant Grotto . . . upon a Bank," while "Soft Musick" provides an obbligato for his pastoral lament:

> Since Love, the brightest Jewel of a Crown,
> That fires Ambition, and adorns Renown;
> That with sweet hopes do's our harsh pains beguil,
> And, midst of Javelins makes the Souldier smile;
> Since this great Trophies lost, quite lost to me,
> What wretched things must fame, and Empire be?[2]

Love has defeated honor. Massinissa's nephew Massina tells him that he is much altered ("Alas! / You look like wither'd Flowers, or Mountain grass."), only to be answered with the line that in its inarticulate suspiration, its denial of words for feeling, seems the acme of sentimental passion and sentimental rhetoric: "O Sophonisba, oh!" His lengthier rhapsodies are crowded with a new sensuousness which attempts to *realize* the physical immediacy of love. Almanzor's appetite for Almahide is openly sexual, of course, but his language never tries to make the same appeal to the audience's senses as does Massinissa's description of his conduct with Sophonisba:

> What furious fires did my hot Nerves invade:
> With open arms upon my Bliss I ran,
> With pangs I grasp'd her like a dying man;
> Like light and heat, incorporate we lay,
> We blest the night, and curst the coming day.
>
> . . . .
>
> Soon as the Birds did on the morning call,
> Her brighter eyes a show'r of tears let fall.
> Which in my panting bosom trickl'd down;
> She prest me close, and cry'd must you be gone?

2. I.117–122. All quotations from Lee's plays are from *The Works of Nathaniel Lee,* ed. Thomas B. Stroup and Arthur L. Cooke, 2 vols. (New Brunswick, N.J., 1954–55); from Otway's, from *The Works of Thomas Otway,* ed. J. C. Ghosh, 2 vols. (Oxford, 1932).

Then round my neck her snowy arms did twine,
She sigh'd; but will you be for ever mine?
Will you be true?—and then our lips did join.

(I.237–241, 244–250)

The plot in which Massinissa is a principal hinges on the necessity for his either losing the beloved Sophonisba by handing her over to her enemy Scipio or losing the friendship of Scipio, his ally and commander. In this dilemma, his personal force and authority can burst free only at moments: his energies are engrossed by his passions. As the sympathetic Lelius comments: "Frail Prince! how wavering all his actions be, / By passions toss'd in Love's tempestuous Sea?" (I. 315–316.) Because his great spirit has turned completely in upon itself, he has lost all genuine autonomy of action. His diction, which displays him, suffers thereby from predictable *mal de mer.*

Without becoming more natural in actuality, the language begins to express, not a state of being, but a process of subjective perception, and appears more "natural" by implying that the speaker stands in a "natural" relation to the world about him, responding to it in some plausible way instead of using it as a stimulus for a new announcement of his integrity. In this fashion, Lee's extravagant diction often differs from high heroic fustian. Although this distinction is not by any means universally valid, some illustration of what I mean may be useful. When Almanzor is brought in, bound and guarded, in *The Conquest of Granada,* Part I, Act V, Scene ii, he learns that surrendering his love will buy his life. He reproaches Almahide and commands his guards as follows:

> Would you to save my life, my love betray?
> Here; take me; bind me: carry me away;
> Kill me: I'll kill you if you disobey.   (H4ᵛ; Act V)

Corneille's Massinisse (*Sophonisbe,* IV.iii) speaks at greater length but to the same effect when confronted with the same sort of choice:

> Chargez, chargez-moi donc de vos fers en sa place:
> Au lieu d'un conquérant par vos mains couronné,
> Trainez à votre Rome un vainqueur enchainé.
> Je suis à Sophonisbe, et mon amour fidèle
> Dédaigne et diadème et liberté sans elle; . . .

In both these cases, we feel that the situation has illuminated the personality—or rather, the nature, for high heroic drama does not distinguish personality from nature—of the speaker, Almanzor or Massinisse. In Lee we find a similar speech:

> Pronounce my death, cut off these cursed hands,
> Send me to Syphax [the enemy], bound
>   with shameful bands.
> That I may all the subtlest torments bear,
> And after death no more reproaches hear.   (II.i.135–138)

Beneath the superficial similarity, there is the immediately noticeable difference that Massinissa evidently is tormented by "reproaches." A look at the context reveals that shortly before this speech he has compared giving up Sophonisba to being run through, so that "your steel smoaks with my hearts reeking Gore" (II.i.37), and then threatened to kill Scipio for continuing the painful subject; immediately after this, leaving his nephew ("My all, the darling of my Soul") as a hostage causes him to break into tears. In short, the quoted speech in this context expresses a state of mind and not a total nature; fustian demonstrates not the integrity, but the disruption of the hero.

Massinissa is the male protagonist of *Sophonisba*, and thus his unheroic conduct is thrown into particular prominence, but it is unique only in degree. Hannibal has given "the World away" for the pleasures of "Melting at Capua" with his mistress Rosalinda, of whom his lieutenant, Maherbal, exclaims: "Grudge you the World? cou'd I such hearts subdue, / Were I great Jove himself I'd give Heaven too" (I.104–107). Scipio abrogates his quest for glory after the mutual suicide of Massinissa and Sophonisba, and decides for rural retirement to "study not to live, but how to die" (V.434). Massina abandons his youthful ambition in Act II so as to dog Rosalinda as a lovelorn page, asking her to "Permit me as your Menial Servant stay, / And near your Person sigh my life away" (III.ii.33–34). When she bids him "eternally Adieu," he resolves to "lay me down" "Near to some murmuring brook . . . ; / Whose waters if they too shallow flow, / My tears shall swell 'em up that I will drown" (III.ii. 44–46). Less than a hundred lines later, he stabs himself for love. In each case, heroic self-aggrandizement is in some way depreciated. Whatever the specific moral of *Sophonisba* may be, whatever balance or reciprocity between reason and passion Lee may have intended, it is quite obvious what sort of emotional effect these characters and these scenes are supposed to have. At the end of the play (V.424), an explicit plea for tears is given to Scipio's lieutenant, Lelius: "What cruel eyes could pity here refrain . . . ?" The plea is implicit throughout.

It would be untrue to imply that *Sophonisba* is only sentimental. On the contrary, all three warriors are given resounding, indeed bombastic, rants. Hannibal, who rants most and best, has

> Made Nature start to see us root up Rocks,
> And open all her adamantine Locks.
> Shake off her massy Barrs, or'e mountains go
> Through Globes of Ice, and flakes of solid Snow.

> (I.10–13)

Scipio proclaims to Massinissa, with lofty mien and pronominal confusion, "I shine above thee like a Star fix'd higher, / Whom though you cannot reach, you may admire" (II.i.99–100). And Massinissa, despite the dulling effects of his melancholy situation on his natural hubris, can still declare, for instance, that

> As Lovers, big with expectation, burn[,]
> My Soul to Battle, do's all fiery turn,
> Swift as the Gods, in hast out strip the wind,
> And leave the Courses of the day behind.

> (I.309–312)

The concerns—love and honor, reason and passion, the external blocking force, greatness of spirit—are those of Dryden's and Settle's and Boyle's earlier work. Lee's language maintains the heroic level, and the characters should be judged by the same criteria of worth as their predecessors. *Sophonisba* is certainly a heroic play in form, and even, partially, in function.

However, even apart from the pervasive, if not yet omnipresent, sentimentality, and from the open desertion of the ideals of glory for the raptures of love, Lee has altered heroic structure in two important ways. The first is that he has resolved the main plot with his hero's suicide, which is totally novel in the heroic play. Even if the historical Massinissa had killed himself, such a resolution would have been curious: why should Lee choose such a story to dramatize? In fact, Massinissa's suicide is purely Lee's invention; the historical Massinissa, as Hofmann's *Lexicon Universale* (1677) gravely informs us: "nonagesimo aetatis anno filium [genuit, et] reliquit liberos, ex diversis uxoribus, quadraginta." The metamorphosis of this Numidian Dorimant into the distressed lover of *Sophonisba* illustrates the stylization of history that we saw at work in Edward Howard's *Usurper* and might see in any one of a number of heroic plays. But to distort history for the sake of a suicide indicates a radical twisting of the heroic form. What Lee has done is to merge the traits of his hero, Massinissa, with the traits of what was a standard secondary character of heroic tragedy, the "friend," who can neither get the heroine nor rid himself of his love for her. Nonantious (*The Heroick-Lover*), Zanger (*Mustapha*), Acacis (*The Indian-Queen*), and Massina (*Sophonisba*) exemplify the type. Since the "friend" has a virtue that is tamer, more exact, than the hero's, he can focus attention on his sufferings without danger of distracting anyone from the hero's achievements. In merging this role with that of the hero, Lee tempers his boldness with caution, accentuating hitherto subordinate traits and softening previous emphases so as not to shock his audience too much.

The second of Lee's innovations also arises from novelty of

stress rather than from revolutionary dramatic technique. This is the splitting of the hero into three—Massinissa, Scipio, and Hannibal—so that each, from a different perspective, mirrors the other two. We have seen this sort of arrangement in *The Villain* and *The Fatal Jealousie,* but Lee brought it to the heroic play for the first time, giving Hart, Mohun, and Kynaston almost equivalent parts. One might remark that the presence of these three dashing actors in the King's Company makes Lee's action all the more striking, for Dryden and other earlier heroic authors had resisted what must have been a very strong temptation to give each of the three a heroic part. Instead, while Hart was sustaining the young Montezuma or Almanzor, Mohun and Kynaston performed the Ynca and Acacis, or Abdelmelech and Boabdelin. Undoubtedly one of the attractions of *Sophonisba* to Killigrew and his customers, and probably to Mohun and Kynaston as well, was the redistribution of heroic roles; this could be accomplished only when the strict sense of genre behind the heroic play, which had forbidden such an arrangement, no longer had much power. Not only, then, does *Sophonisba* deflate the preternatural heroism of the hero through making it common, but it also reveals the implicit willingness to accept such a change on the part of the theatrical management and the public.[3]

Sophonisba has been treated as typical of a group of plays, and many—*all* would be too much to hope for—of the same shifts of interest appear in the rest of the group. Lee's love-mad Britannicus (*Nero*), for instance, speaks in similarly unheroic vein about his friend Flavius, who has just bid his heart break at Britannicus' plight:

3. In *The History of Charles the Eighth of France* of another of the newer playwrights, John Crowne, published 1672, four years before *Sophonisba,* there are three heroes, one of whom, the Prince of Salerne, rips the bandages from his wounds and causes his own death rather than be captured. But Crowne's heroes are less differentiated than Lee's, Salerne's suicide is for honor rather than for love, and the principles of heroism are not challenged by dramatic failure.

> Ha! he does weep! nay, pry'thee do not hide it;
> By Heav'n, thou art my friend: lend me thy store;
> My eyes shall pay thee use, trust me they shall;
> Here, in my bosome, lay thy pearly stock;
> Heav'ns, how he weeps! thou art a Virgin sure.
> Fall, you dear drops; Oh let me hug thee close:
> My Spirits are quite parch'd up, my palat's dry;
> Th'Elizian shades are cool: oh, let me dye.   (V.i.29–36)

It is worth noting that even in this heroic play Lee freed Major Mohun from the necessity of trying to be pathetic in couplets: the end-stopped lines are an uncomfortable compromise between the proper rigidity of high decorum and the natural brokenness and flaccidity of passion. Otway's Don Carlos is given a long, lachrymose death scene after having ended an almost equally lachrymose life with suicide, cutting his veins in his bath. The method itself has the taint of decadence, smacking more of the effete Petronius than of Cato. Like Lee's Flavius, King Philip cries out, "Break, break, my heart" (V.368), while his tears flow and Don Carlos' knees tremble (V.347, 357). In the previous act, Carlos has entered to address the Queen in consistent manner:

> . . . Run out of breath by Fate,
> And persecuted by a Fathers hate,
> Weari'd with all, I panting hither fly,
> To lay my self down at your feet and dy.
>
> (IV.345–348)

Otway's first tragedy, *Alcibiades,* presented another hero who commits suicide, dying with:

> But oh!—
> A heavy faintness does each sense surprize:
> Yet e're I close up these unhappy eyes,
> Here their last dutious sorrows they shall pay
> And at this object [Timandra's body] melt
>   in tears away.   (V.480–484)

In describing the protagonist of still another play of this type, Crowne's *The Destruction of Jerusalem* (1677), Maidment and Logan claim that "there is a striking resemblance between the hero of Dryden and the hero of Crowne. Phraartes, the deposed monarch of Parthia, and the lover of Clarona, in both parts of the 'Destruction of Jerusalem,' has all the characteristics of Almanzor, the Drawcansir of the 'Rehearsal,' so much so, that it is not easy to decide whether he or Almanzor deals most in wordy declamation and outrageous bombast."[4] If Phraartes has all Almanzor's characteristics, the reverse is not the case. Almanzor has no speech equivalent in tone to Phraartes' at Clarona's death:

> She dyes!—she dyes!—
> Speak once again! open once more those eyes;
> *Phraartes* speaks to thee!—she's fled—she's fled!—
> And her pale Picture left me in her stead.
> This—this is all of her that I must have—
> And this is too the portion of the Grave.
> Away with tears!—this fond—this womanish floud!—
> One kiss!—and then—to bloud—revenge—and bloud.
>
> (Part II, H3ᵛ; Act V)

After this lament of disjunct phrases, Phraartes briefly goes mad. Like Massinissa, unlike Almanzor, he shares his heroship: Crowne has given the characteristic theme of love and glory to another couple, Titus and Berenice. Here, as in the other late heroic plays—and this is a significant difference between these plays and their predecessors—love and glory are in opposition, an opposition introduced by Lee's *Nero* (1675) and carried through in all the rhymed plays by Lee, Otway, and Crowne after that, as well as in *Aureng-Zebe* (1676). In *The Destruction of Jerusalem*, Crowne resolves the conflict by separating the lovers rather

---

4. John Crowne, *The Dramatic Works with Prefatory Memoir and Notes*, ed. James Maidment and W. H. Logan, 4 vols. (Edinburgh and London, 1873–74), II, 219–220.

than by establishing harmony; the parting scene finds both the martial emperor Titus and Berenice in tears. Banks' *The Rival Kings* (1677) presents still more extreme an alteration of the hero. His Macedonian Alexander and Ephestion call each other "dear" and "dearest Love" (H, H2), and exhaust the last act of the play with sentimental obsequies for one another; they too share their heroic prominence, with Oroondates and Lysimachus.

Although proliferated examples do not prove, they can clarify, specify, the changes of tone and technique in the later heroic play: (1) the new diminution and sentimentalization of the hero, (2) the new resolution of conflicts without either the removal of the blocking forces or a heroic death, (3) the new conflict between love and honor/glory. A fourth shift of emphasis, implied if not in part exemplified in the discussion of *Sophonisba*, develops from (2) and (3). Since the world of aspiration and greatness had begun to spoil, the private life began to be stressed to the exclusion of the public, insofar as the loftiness of the tragic character permitted. For the harmony of private and public in the high heroic play, Lee and the rest offer withdrawal from public life—pastoralism, suicide—or prolonged pessimism, such as we find in Aureng-Zebe's splendid speech beginning "When I consider Life, 'tis all a cheat" (H; Act III). The ideal of innocence takes over from that of prowess, Eden from empire; and here we have what is perhaps a still farther dwelling upon the private life, for the land of heart's desire turns out most of the time to be no more than a dream, never sufficiently public to have existed in the world of fact.

As I pointed out at the end of my discussion of the attacks on rhyme, these changes in the heroic play did not come because the times or the audience changed. The mid-seventies did not embitter or disillusion the public, forcing it to "express itself" by artistic proxy in this new drama. Rather, as soon as the theatre offered the pleasures of vicarious achievement in the spectacular opera, the audience seized the equally sensational pleasures of virtuous compassion in the pathetic play. It is true that the pathetic tragedy is not "libertine" as the old heroic play had been accused of being; that it furthered benevolence as the "affective" critics said; that it glorified gentleness and innocence, those Christian godchildren, rather than social violence; that it rid itself of the odor of impiety that clings to the idea of distorting Nature. But one should be cautious in assuming that the apparent moral superiority of pathetic over heroic drama in any way reflects the actual moral disposition of the audience. The effect of the plays may have been to refine manners and morals in the long run, of course, but that is quite a different matter.

6

LEE, BANKS, OTWAY

FROM THE LATE HEROIC PLAY, THE DEVELOPMENT OF TRAGEDY between about 1675 and 1685 is clear. The three most important dramatists of this period, Lee, Banks, and Otway, set the pace, with a continuing originality that outdid any of their contemporaries. Dryden, who might have exerted as much force upon this tragedy as he had upon heroics, retired from the competition after *All for Love,* "not merely, as it may seem to some, the summit of his achievement in tragedy, but . . . the limit of his experiments in it."[1] And Tate, Settle, Crowne, Southerne—these men showed ingenuity and mechanical skill, nothing more. This importance by default which the tragedies of Lee, Banks, and Otway enjoy becomes still further pronounced when one realizes their influence, for the structure of tragedy changed very little in the last fifteen years of the century, in contrast to the energy of invention and change between 1660 and 1680. The reasons for this stasis were, I think, largely extra-literary: the union of the theatres in 1682 temporarily forced caution and consolidation of gains upon the new monopoly. As George Powell remarked in his preface to *The Treacherous Brothers* (1690), "The time was, upon the uniting of the two *Theatres,* that the revieing of the old stock of Plays, so ingrost the study of the House, that the Poets lay dorment; and a new Play cou'd hardly get admittance, amongst the more precious pieces of Antiquity, that then waited to walk the Stage." During the seven or eight years of this

1. George Saintsbury, introduction to the Mermaid edition of Dryden's *Plays* (reprinted New York, 1957), I, xviii. *Don Sebastian* is a more technically complex and brilliant tragedy than *All for Love,* but it introduces no technical innovations.

discouraging conservatism, Lee went mad and Otway died, so that neither could develop new forms or new complexities; and Dryden and Banks were inactive. Except of course in some individual plays—Dryden's two last tragedies, *The Mourning Bride,* perhaps one or two others—English tragedy was exhausted by these circumstances, and until almost the turn of the century, lay tamely within forms established by Lee, Banks, and Otway.

Lee changed less than either Banks or Otway, and in him we may see the refinement of the possibilities that the late heroic play held forth. One can indicate the direction of these refinements neatly, if factitiously, by looking at the first lines of some of Lee's plays. The heroic plays begin as one might expect: "Conquest with Laurels has our arms adorn'd" (*Sophonisba*), "Vast are the Glories, Caesar, thou hast won" (*Gloriana*), fighting between Hephestion and Lysimachus in his first unrhymed tragedy, *The Rival Queens.* The lamentation that begins *Nero* has a specific political source. By the time we get to *Mithridates* we find a passionate love lament, though still with a specified source; and *Oedipus* opens not with words, but with "a plaintive Tune, representing the present condition of Thebes; Dead Bodies appear at a distance in the Streets; Some faintly go over the Stage, others drop." Visual sensationalism precedes verbal reasoning. Minor characters then describe for the next forty lines the effect of the plague upon Thebes, stressing its irrationality and horror. (Sophocles, in contrast, begins with the confident Oedipus himself; Corneille, with love disputes; Seneca, with introspection.)

Passionate love, driven beyond ordinary heroic intensity, and vagueness of powerful feeling perhaps come to a head in the first speech of *Lucius Junius Brutus.* Lee's rhetoric here anticipates ideas of the psychological sublime that flower in Burke:

> *Titus.* O Teraminta, why this face of tears?
> Since first I saw thee, till this happy day,

Thus hast thou past thy melancholly hours,
Ev'n in the Court retir'd; stretch'd on a bed
In some dark room, with all the Cortins drawn;   5
Or in some Garden o're a Flowry bank
Melting thy sorrows in the murmuring Stream;
Or in some pathless Wilderness a musing,
Plucking the mossy bark of some old Tree,
Or poring, like a Sybil, on the Leaves;   10
What, now the Priest should joyn us! O, the Gods!
What can you proffer me in vast exchange
For this ensuing night? Not all the days
Of Crowning Kings, of Conquering Generals,
Not all the expectation of hereafter;   15
With what bright Fame can give in th' other World
Should purchase thee this night one minute from me.

The first line of the play begins with a suspiration and ends
with "tears." The three images of retirement grow progressively
wilder, more ominous, and so, more intriguing, from the cur-
tained room to the garden to the "pathless Wilderness," increasing the audience's interest. In no case does Lee become specific
about place: "some dark room," "some Garden o're a Flowry
bank," "some pathless Wilderness," "some old Tree." All objects
are connotative only. And we may see still more with the help of
Burke: "The truth is, if poetry gives us a noble assemblage of
words, corresponding to many noble ideas, which are connected
by circumstances of time and place, or related to each other as
cause and effect, or associated in any natural way, they may be
moulded together in any form, and perfectly answer their
end. The picturesque [i.e., imagistic] connection is not
demanded . . ."[2] If for "noble," one reads "pathetic," Lee's prin-

2. Edmund Burke, *A Philosophical Enquiry into the Origin of our Ideas of
the Sublime and Beautiful,* ed. J. T. Boulton (London and New York, 1958),
p. 171. In the context—Burke's discussion of words and "sensible images"— my "imagistic" accurately reflects the meaning of Burke's "picturesque." Burke's use of the word is not Gilpin's.
I am using Burke because his analysis of poetry helps one to talk about Lee,

ciples of dramatic rhetoric (and those of Lee's contemporaries) become much clearer. Visual imagery refers to percepts rather than merely to objects. The verse clings to the connotative world in the minds of the audience rather than to the created world of the drama, as the language moves out to its public and the empathetic public moves into the play. It follows that the arrangement of Lee's rhetoric need result from no inner compulsion, either of the movement of the language itself or of the psychology of the speaker. There is no personal reason for Titus to arrange the room/garden/wilderness images in that order; nor are we supposed to imagine that Titus has personally discovered Teraminta plucking mossy bark or melting her sorrows (if we were, his complacency and naïveté at this point would go well beyond what even the clumsy conventions of exposition permit)—these are just iconographic actions.

Furthermore, the logical movement of the passage is bolstered by a rigid formal structure that actually stylizes Titus' speech into units of feeling for ready presentation, while seeming to build up momentum within his passionate expression. The three temporal expressions in lines 2 and 3 fall into two half-lines and a full line, with "melancholly hours" balancing "happy day." Then, we get two pairs of lines and a set of three lines, expressing parallel examples of retirement, the first pair made up of distinct half-lines in which "Cortins" in the last half echoes "Court" in the first; the next pair makes the caesuras less open, but balances the halves by grammatical parallelism, line 6, and alliteration, line 7. Anaphora connects lines 8 and 10 with 6; alliteration on "p," lines 8, 9, and 10 with one another; line 8 has one element, 9 has two, 10, three. "Sybil" in line 10 then leads to "Priest" and "Gods" in line 11, which in turn is joined to line 12

---

not because Lee's plays are seventy-five years ahead of their time. There is, of course, an historical connection: pathetic tragedy and its rhetoric influenced the criticism of Dennis and Addison, which directly and indirectly (through its effect on non-dramatic poetry) helped influence Burke. But I am not stressing that historical connection here, important and neglected as I think it is.

by the repetition of "What," in two different syntactic functions, and the picking up of the sounds of "Priest" and "Gods" in "proffer," a connection of sound that the sense of the lines makes sharp. Then we have once more four half-lines balanced (night/days; Of Crowning Kings/of Conquering Generals) followed by a full line linked to them by sense and anaphora, and two half-lines, 16, roughly parallel in syntax, followed by a full line that is tied to 16 by the rhyming contrast between "bright" and "night," and the somewhat less obvious one between "World" and "purchase." To go on with this analysis would be tedious—what I want to make plain is that Lee's verse is carefully constructed in abstract forms, as Fletcher's is, and that these forms supplant imagery as a central principle of ordering the verse. Or, to put this another way, instead of a means of ordering in which the content and structure of the verse refer to the work of art, Lee provides means in which content refers directly to the feelings of the audience, outside the verse, and the structure refers to equally external patterns of arrangement, based on syntax.

The illusion, however, is of the natural, and in keeping with this, Lee makes full use of the prose rabble scenes about which I spoke in discussing the unrhymed plays of the earlier Restoration. I will remain with *Lucius Junius Brutus* for convenience' sake. Here Lee assigned the role of plebeian leader Vinditius to the great comedian James Nokes, and permitted him to ask whether Tarquin can "make our Pots boil, tho the Davil piss in the Fire" and to call Fabritius the "Crack-fart of the Court." Fabritius in turn warns against speeches in which "the words lye like a low Wrestler, round, close and short, squat, pat and pithy" (II.i.47–48; 71; 27–28). As in plays like *Andronicus Comnenius* (rather than *The Villain*), this level of style remains completely discrete from the other. While a Renaissance playwright's range of styles suggests social continuity, Lee's reinforces hierarchy. It safeguards at least a reminiscence of heroic speech and heroic virtues in the formal "naturalness" of Titus and Teraminta. Lee thus makes up for the rants that he cannot write.

He makes up for most of the rest of the extravagance of the heroic play with a new dose of sensationalism. There are scenes of human sacrifice—goblets of blood, crucifixion, burning, shrieks (IV.i)—of Titus bloody from whipping and Teraminta "Defil'd and mangled" (V.i), of headless bodies (V.ii). There is sexual openness: "When words are at a loss, and the mute Soul / Pours out her self in sighs and gasping joys" (I.i); or Titus' announcement of his impotence (IV.i); or Lucius Junius Brutus' extraordinary reference (I.i.215) to the "slimy joys" of marriage. Lee also provides liberal servings of pathos, with much sighing and weeping, including that of a child whose "pretty eyes [are] ruddy and wet with tears, / Like two burst Cherries rowling in a storm" (V.ii.100–101), and several times the weeping of Brutus himself, although Livy and Plutarch speak only of his toughness. Titus, like a still further debilitated Massinissa, is kept in almost constant hysteria throughout the tragedy, driven through melancholy, joy, despair, fear, shame, and general mental anguish; Lee only pardons Titus when he can be left exhausted like a squeezed sponge in the flow of passion, to soak in enough energy for fresh exploitation.

Titus is not Protean as are Fletcher's characters, for the heroic and pathetic insistence upon the individual character is too strong to permit that. He achieves the same sort of effect, however, by being so frail that event after event blows him to varying extremes and destroys any chance he might have had to show a single personality. The ideals of love and honor, Teraminta and Brutus, remain as constant as in the days of heroics, but now they are personified in the world, not enshrined within the hero. As in no heroic play, these two conflicting ideals are concentrated so as to become more demanding, purified so as to emphasize their simple existence outside the hero. At the same time

Lee counterbalances one's sense that Teraminta and Brutus are to be seen only in relation to Titus and to Titus' conflicting aspirations. He makes them human and sympathetic, letting them share in the pathos and thus dividing the dramatically central position of the hero.

In Banks we find a different approach to very much the same sort of thing. While the late rhyming hero had to be reduced in stature by the device of introducing other heroes, Banks' "she-tragedies" shift so much weight to the heroine, and display heroes who are so woefully ineffective, that no artifices for reducing them are needed. Along these lines Banks created a new staple character for Restoration tragedy, the stupid hero. No one, I suppose, could claim that Muly Hamet and Almanzor are Aristotles in buskins, but at least they are not blatantly foolish or naïve. Banks' heroes are both, beginning with Achilles (*The Destruction of Troy*), and proceeding through Essex (*The Unhappy Favourite*), Piercy (*Vertue Betray'd*), and especially Norfolk (*The Island Queens*). These men cannot think, though they feel immensely; they resemble those monumental figures of Henry Moore's, carved with huge smooth bodies and infinitesimal heads. Each is allowed some harmless impetuosity, the last rags of lost virility; but in fact they can only live, like Banks' women, in sad religiose patience, rejecting greatness, suffering betrayal as a sure anticipation of death. As one critic remarks: "From the weakness of the person and the strength of conscience proceeds the essential quality of patient suffering, the complete surrender to a destiny that can be endured in exemplary fashion with a glance toward the hereafter and the help that can only come, be it now or later, from heaven."[3] Within this context, no one can be surprised to find the distinction between male and female characters, which is at the heart of the heroic play, almost obliterated in Banks. This is even true in terms of stage action:

3. Hans Hochuli, *John Banks: Eine Studie zum Drama des späten 17. Jahrhunderts* . . . , Swiss Studies in English, No. 32 (Bern, 1952), p. 84.

Banks is given to having men kiss in his plays.[4] More essentially, he alters the received structure of tragedy by having the lovers victimized together, in the three plays of the eighties, without differentiating by sex the nature of the life that they might choose. The love and honor open to Lee's Titus are not those open to Teraminta; in a Banks tragedy, they would be substantially the same.

Consequently, Banks goes farther than Lee in downgrading honor, the more masculine of the perpetual antitheses. One can see this even in the huffing *The Destruction of Troy,* in which Achilles falls so head-over-heels in love with Polyxena that he offers to (*a*) lie next to Troilus' corpse until it returns to life, (*b*) submit to being stabbed, and (*c*) submit to being dragged around the walls of Troy. In each of these, of course, he puts himself in the place of one of his victims, as love takes over the functions of honor. Appropriately enough, he dies at the marriage altar. It is true that in this play the Greeks pledge to fight for "Virtue, Property, . . . Credit, [and] Fame" (B3), and the impending combat between Achilles and Hector is spoken of in terms that include "ambitious Glory" (C3ᵛ), but honor as an ideal, as a motive, as *the* motive, cannot be taken seriously. Love and friendship are taken seriously, and what honor there is must be construed in terms of these personal ideals. Personal relations had always been, and continued to be, women's province: dwelling upon them gives us Banks' she-tragedies, in which women are the principals and the men are womanish.

The domesticity demanded by several of the critics discussed in Chapter 1 comes easily to Banks in his constant, often successful, hunt for pathos. Domesticity in turn led him to make his second contribution to dramatic history—the first being the she-tragedy—with the return to English themes. I do not think that he was motivated here either by a desire to use familiar

4. Achilles and Patroclus (*The Destruction of Troy*), Alexander and Hephestion (*The Rival Kings*), and Cyrus and Croesus (*Cyrus the Great*) kiss; Norfolk and Cecil (*The Island Queens*) merely embrace.

stories or by chauvinism, as was, for instance, John Caryll in *The English Princess* earlier in the Restoration. What Banks wanted was an assurance of probability.[5] In his dedication to *Vertue Betray'd* (1682), he rebukes "poets, who may think it an easier Course to write of the Improbable and Romantick Actions of Princes remote, both by distance of Time and Place . . ." The near and the probable, he felt, were in direct proportion, and English history therefore guaranteed him a measure of "Nature," that new golden booty, just as the use of semi-mythic Oriental or Turkish history had guaranteed the heroic playwrights the exoticism, the extravagance, the opulence that went into the brewing of admiration. One can look at the matter in a different way by distinguishing the magnanimity excited through the heroic hero from the benevolence excited through his pathetic counterpart. Since the audience in the former case learns to be self-regarding, the more general the myth of the play the better; but benevolence requires at least the illusion of a specific response to a specific person or persons, and therefore turns to the particular as well as to the domestic. Here, again, Banks' use of English history served him, and encouraged him to place an unusual emphasis on the vital context that surrounds his characters.

As usual, the simultaneous appeal to passion and nature produces a highly rhetorical, superficially simple, diction. Banks avoids prose—he has no rabble scenes, for instance—and thereby deprives himself of any sort of generic decorum with which to brace his style. As a result, he slips about badly in his blank verse, justifying Lessing's remark: "He is at the same time so ordinary and so precious, so low and so bombastic, and that not from person to person but all throughout, that he can serve as a sample of this kind of heterogeneity."[6] For a playwright of Banks' obvious limitations, writing within the dramatic context

5. David S. Berkeley, "Some Notes on Probability in Restoration Drama," *Notes and Queries*, CC (1955), 237–239, 342–344, 432, discusses and richly documents the connections of the domestic and the probable.

6. Quoted by Hochuli, *John Banks*, p. 79.

of the early 1680's, the rabble scene simply would have scraped across the grain of his tragedy, raising by contrast the language that Banks was working so hard to lower. As Lessing's comment suggests, he pays for his limitations, falls into difficulty, and cushions himself at last resort with the advice that Anna Bullen (*Vertue Betray'd*) gives her daughter: "Strive not for Words, my Child; these little drops / Are far more Eloquent than Speech can be—" (L; Act V). More to Banks' purpose is the rant, which he revives for his villains to make them the measures of adverse destiny. Not only does villains' rant make the hero's and heroine's speeches more domestic—rather than more temperate, as in *Aureng-Zebe*—but also, through its categorizing function, it gives villainy an important purity and objectivity. While *Lucius Junius Brutus* personifies the hero's choice between love and honor, in Teraminta and Brutus respectively, Banks' plays personify the cruel impositions of the world upon its sufferers. Since there is only one value, love, choice becomes irrelevant, and the villains that Lee can exclude re-enter the scene.

Otway, the third and greatest of the new playwrights, joins forces with Lee and Banks in a number of ways, although in detailed intelligence of execution he surpasses both of them as well as every other serious dramatist of the Restoration, Dryden perhaps excluded. In considering his tragedies, as in considering Dryden's, one should not slough aside the seemingly extrinsic fact that both wrote comedies. Dryden's experience in comedy led him to calibrate his boldness in his heroic plays. Cibber's discussion of Kynaston's rodomontade as Morat illuminates this point brilliantly. Quoting Morat's riposte to Nourmahal's demand that Aureng-Zebe not be spared, "I'll do't, to shew my Arbitrary Power," Cibber writes, *"Risum teneatis?* It was impossible not to laugh and reasonably too, when this Line came out of the Mouth of *Kynaston*, with the stern and haughty Look that attended it." He goes on to say that such reasonable laughter as Kynaston elicited, "doubtless not without *Dryden's* Approbation," was not the laughter of ridicule but that of judgment, which witnesses and approves the handling of heroic decorum.[7] We can see how closely analogous such pleasure is to the pleasure of watching the comic hero triumph in fulfilling his own nature, verbally and in action. The greater the daring within the proper limits of the genre, the better for delighting us, and for fixing the boundaries of genre and character both.

We do not find this technique in Boyle, but it becomes one of Dryden's most important devices for controlling the decorum of his heroic plays; and, despite the sporadic appearance of gambits from Restoration comedy—Indamora's feminine rule over her suitor Arimant, for instance—it remains the most important technical borrowing from comedy in the heroic play. Settle seizes on the same device in *The Empress of Morocco*, using it more blatantly. But the early plays of Otway, Banks, and Lee, in which unbounded intensities of passion were gulped down on faith, had to discard this rule of proportion, a rule of literary artifice rather than of nature. We have seen the results: Banks' simplification and Lee's eclectic use of sensationalism, the rabble scene, tension built up through forcing the hero through a gauntlet of impossible choices. Lee tries, roughly speaking, to reconstruct within the new forms the elements of the heroic play, while Banks tends to pare all inconveniences away. With his consciousness professionally attuned to the forms of Restoration comedy, Otway shapes his two late tragedies in other, dramatically more fruitful, ways.

The Orphan (1680) turns on the idea of Nature, largely in the terms in which Restoration comedy had explored that idea. Naturalistic comedy governs its content, though not its form. After the stunningly inept exposition of Ernesto and Paulino, which hastily sets up the situation, Otway proceeds to his task. He develops and tests the sexual cynicism familiar to audiences

7. Cibber, *Apology*, I, 123–125. Cibber also quotes Addison's agreement "that even Tragedy on such particular Occasions might admit of a *Laugh of Approbation*." The importance of precise decorum, of whatever sort, to the Restoration audience could not be more clearly illuminated.

of Etherege and Wycherley. Castalio's permitting Polydore to make love to Monimia runs parallel to the Harcourt-Sparkish-Alithea subplot of *The Country Wife;* his embarrassment at marriage comes straight from the comedies ("When I am old and weary of the World, / I may grow desperate / And take a Wife to mortify withall" [I.163–165]), even to the rhythms of the wit. Polydore, the rake, ends the first act with an attack on hypocritic virtue, inconstant women, and the inability of men to act like "the lusty Bull" who enjoys his female "and abandons her at Will." Later, in Act III, he displays Dorimant-like malice in his glee over an intriguing mistress "that has wit to charm the very Soul, / And give a double relish to delight!" (419–426.) Even Monimia shares the cynicism, more mildly but most oddly, given her lifetime of Bohemian seclusion: "[I'll] Be a true Woman, rail, protest my wrongs, / Resolve to hate him, and yet love him still" (I.278–279). Perhaps she gets it from her brother Chamont, who announces to her that men "are by Nature false, / Dissembling, subtle, cruel, and unconstant" (II.288–289), or perhaps from any other character in the play, for they all share the same lace-cuffed Hobbesianism about matters of love. The pastoral setting offers no protection from the corrupt nature which skulks within it, or rather, which the characters have induced within it by their beliefs. *The Orphan* is not a Lee-like tragedy of choice or a Banksian tragedy of oppression, but a tragedy of the imagination, in which nature becomes vicious because the characters, like those in Restoration comedy, assume that it was vicious to begin with.

Within the tragedy, the standing belief in corrupt nature crystallizes in distrust: each of the protagonists comes to disaster because he fails to trust the others. This Restoration comedy view makes Castalio hesitant about owning his marriage and accounts for his otherwise excessive misery when he thinks that Monimia has barred him from consummation. His grief at broken faith turns out to be self-regarding, as the emotions of a young Hobbesian might logically be, and as the emotions of

Polydore of course are. With this in mind, one might speculate that Otway's choice of title refers to more than poor pathetic unprotected Monimia. Every character seems isolated, orphaned, from every other, as Otway continues throughout to dissolve the family gathering, so harmonious at the beginning of Act I, only to reconstruct it later in the irony of his ending, when the family must re-establish trust in their deadly news. Not only does *The Orphan* secure that isolation upon which pathos ordinarily thrives, but it also seems to rebuke the blending of naturalism and individual romance that makes up Restoration comedy, and in another way, the heroic play. The logic of their assumptions, Otway shows, ruins the felicity of their conclusions, which unite hero and society. *The Orphan* insists upon its difference from these earlier plays, its reasonable naturalness as opposed to their romance, and thus defines its subject matter by contrast as Dryden had defined his genre by analogy.

But Otway blends the outside world with the individual in another way from that of the heroic play: as Lee and Banks make psychological forces objective, so Otway projects psychology into the world. He does this through symbolism. Let us look first at Chamont's prophetic dream. He sees his sister Monimia defiled in a sort of perversely erotic dream that foreshadows the incest in the play. Otway amplifies the implication by having Chamont wake to find his sword piercing the pictured story of Oedipus' parricide (II.222–237). Rationally, one must admit that the dream would be more appropriate for Polydore or Castalio, who more closely manage to involve themselves with incest and a father's death or near death. Otway appears to be yielding to a particularly sloppy way of tying subplot and main plot together while darkening his tragedy with that fog of generalized evil that we discussed in relationship to Fletcher. But dramatically, Chamont, Castalio, and Polydore are so plainly variations on the same character that such displacement does not seem intrusive, and helps to make objective the oppressions of fate within the play—the technique reminds one of Banks' and Lee's objectifying of oppressive forces. Another such clear objective symbol is the sybilline woman whom Chamont has met, dressed as she is in the colors of the apocalypse ("different colour'd Rags, black, red, white, yellow" [II.255]): she is real but has as well a mythical flavor, so that she is continuous with the more subjective dream on the one side and with the more objective reality of the play on the other. The sybilline woman, with her ominous seed of fear, helps join thought and action as the objectifying of the dream does. A last example is the boar hunt, which begins quite in the world of reality, and suggests a manly co-operation in slaying rage and passion, the usual classical meaning of the boar. But by the beginning of the second act, when Acasto enters to tell of his having killed a second boar, the brothers have already moved from one kind of venery to the other. Thus Acasto has killed the second boar alone, and stands alone as the source of virtue. Within this framework, his sickness at the beginning of Act III, as his sons slip from his standards, is not padding but symbol. So is his distemper that opens Act IV. Otway's criterion of inclusion has to do with the hero's way of feeling, not with the simple narrative line or, as in the heroic play, with the hero's show of prowess.

One can see the same sort of thing in Otway's second, and greater, tragedy, *Venice Preserv'd*.[8] Here the seedy and sinister conspirators of the earlier acts can die like men, "Worthy their Character," without real inconsistency. Our perceptions of their actions cannot be divorced from Jaffeir's state at the moment; all actions in the play are functions, in a quasi-mathematical sense,

---

8. William H. McBurney, "Otway's Tragic Muse Debauched: Sensuality in *Venice Preserv'd*," *Journal of English and Germanic Philology*, LVIII (1959), 380–399, also discusses the effects upon Otway's tragedy of his experience in writing comedy. I have not documented specific points of agreement or disagreement with McBurney's article, to which I am indebted; see also Aline Mackenzie Taylor, *Next to Shakespeare: Otway's "Venice Preserv'd" and "The Orphan" and Their History on the London Stage* (Durham, 1950), pp. 39–72, and David R. Hauser, "Otway Preserved: Theme and Form in *Venice Preserv'd*," SP, LV (1958), 481–493.

of Jaffeir's suffering. The conspirators must be unpalatable in Act III, gallant in Act V, because their virtue and vice are contingent, not absolute. When Almanzor truly boasts, probably to his creator's ironic amusement, that Almahide must be chaste because she's loved by him, he refers to generic patterns in which he knows his supreme and yet determined place; when Jaffeir's world writhes in hostility about him, a new reciprocity has arisen in which world and character seem to shape each other and generic patterns seem to have faded before more lifelike and less univocal kinds of order. In one sense, of course, the environment of the pathetic hero is very much like that of his heroic counterpart, for it is designed to show off the captivating prowess of the hero. His feelings are fanned out like a peacock's tail. Furthermore, if the pathetic world has grown more impervious and inexorable, it shows itself so singly from the hero's point of view that the new losses and gains of control more or less balance each other out, and give us as firm an equilibrium as we get in the heroic play. Empathy makes public the hero's subjectivity, and becomes a principle of form.

The active counterpart of the shaping point of view about which I have been talking, is the attempt by the hero to manufacture order for himself. His attempts are almost always conventional—marriage, the family, patriotism—but the pathetic play tries to give at least the impression that these impositions of order upon a hostile environment are choices, and not, as in the heroic play, *données*. The failure of these attempts in *The Orphan* logically occasions Castalio's curse:

> Confusion and disorder seize the World,
> To spoyl all trust and converse amongst men;
> 'Twixt Families ingender endless fewds,
> In Countrys needless fears, in Cities factions,
> In States Rebellion, and in Churches Schism:
> Till all things move against the course of Nature;
> Till Form's dissolv'd, the Chain of Causes broken,
> And the Originals of Being lost.   (V.502–509)

In the hands of a poor dramatist, this sort of stuff is rant; in the hands of an Otway, it makes sense, for it involves the recognition that the simple order by which Castalio has attempted to live is metonymous for much more sweeping kinds of order. This is not because, as in *King Lear,* hierarchies of order are implicit in the play, but because with the simple orders of marriage and family Castalio has gone as far as the limits of his power permit.

Jaffeir's case seems still more desperate, for he is afflicted not only by the timidity of a Castalio but also by implacable external forces. Like Lee's and even Banks' heroes, Jaffeir finds himself driven to a hysteria of commitment, pledging himself intensely if inconstantly to any promise of order. The complexity of his characterization within this typical framework—his alternations of cynicism and tearful fidelity, indifference, enthusiasm, coward-ice, and rationalization—goes far beyond anything that Lee or Banks could do, and owes its fineness to Otway's genius and to his experience in writing about natural and non-tragic emotions.

Nowhere can this fineness be better seen than in Otway's psychological handling of the eroticism pervasive in all the trage-dies of this time, both as a sensational element to compensate for the loss of heroic flamboyance and as an index of intense per-sonal feeling. A love that joins the joys of body and spirit seems the least intricate of orders by which a man can live, and it becomes the central value of the precarious world that Restora-tion tragedy reveals. So it is, implicitly, in *The Orphan.* But in *Venice Preserv'd,* Otway begins by twining love with infidelity, Jaffeir's betrayal of Priuli's friendship and hospitality. Here Jaf-feir's moral condition takes root: although the moral importance of Jaffeir's acts must be, on one level, dubious—after all, nothing he does can make much difference, given the structure of reality outside him—our sense of his integrity, as well as his own, governs that single province over which he has some control, the province of sympathy. For the love-and-honor heroes, apparently conflicting demands keep coming up at one moment or another, but the sense of values that copes with the conflicts can retain its sanctity. This is true even in Lee and Banks. But for Jaffeir, whose acts of choice are isolated and illuminated precisely because they have lost effective meaning in the world and can spin freely—for Jaffeir all choice is tainted. The unhappy decision between corrupt senate and corrupt conspiracy merely echoes in the outer world his inner choice of guilt toward Belvidera or guilt toward friendship. To keep Belvidera, without whom he cannot live, means enjoying the wrong to Priuli, and in these terms the conspiracy means to Jaffeir the chance to project his own guilt upon the senate. His alternations of glee and horror at the prospect suggest that he realizes how he is about to redeem his honor, through butchery conceived in a whore's house or at midnight upon the Rialto, symbolizing his own darkest and most prostituted feelings. Otway extenuates this fact, which he yet has no wish to annul. For this reason, Belvidera, on whose behalf Jaffeir had been stimulated to join the conspiracy, must be surrendered to it. She is the token of Jaffeir's earlier betrayal of friendship, and therefore his anxiety to show his fidelity to the conspirators leads him to deliver her *en déshabillée* to Renault and Bedamar.

Within this paradoxical situation, the subplot takes on new meaning. R. E. Hughes has astutely observed that the comedy acts as a corollary, as well as a complement, to the tragic action. "The play is, in effect, an extended double-take, a grim and oppressive version of the comic scenes between Antonio and Aquilina."[9] Venice is not only sordid, as the comedy proves, but expressly sordid under the skin: the act of seeing the ugliness beneath the slapstick in the subplot duplicates the act of seeing the ugliness in senate, conspirators, one's love, and oneself. In other words, a paradox of delight and disgust becomes a universal metaphor for the process of moral perception. We perform in our minds, watching the subplot, the same mental procedure as

9. R. E. Hughes, " 'Comic Relief' in Otway's *Venice Preserv'd*," *N&Q*, CCIII (1958), 66. I carry my psychological reading of the play further than Mr. Hughes would, I think; he treats the three principals as innocents.

do the characters, watching (from within) the tragic action. Even Antonio's perverted return to the simple state, the beast with asocial impulses, plays upon the pastoralism of Jaffeir and Belvidera, and Pierre's cry for primal liberty. The natural and unnatural are entwined. In these moral and psychological terms, Otway recasts the traditional role of Belvidera, at once Jaffeir's highest good and the enemy of his honor. He also recasts the tin idol Nature, whose ambivalence, already suggested, dominates Belvidera's final mad speeches. After cursing all natural things, "herb and fruit and tree," "the rain that falls upon the earth," "man and beast," she crazily re-establishes natural bonds and stylized natural beauty:

> What? to my husband then conduct me quickly,
> Are all things ready? shall we dye most gloriously?
> Say not a word of this to my old father,
> Murmuring streams, soft shades, and springing flowers,
> Lutes, Laurells, Seas of Milk, and ships of Amber.
>   (V.351–353, 365–369)

Jaffeir's "reading" of the scenes with Antonio constitutes another level of meaning. Encouraged by Pierre, he sees Antonio's relationship with Aquilina as an exaggeration of Priuli's unnatural assault upon Belvidera, both using senatorial privilege and pocketbook. Pierre employs this analogy to inflame Jaffeir, and also to exculpate his Aquilina by comparing her with the angelic Belvidera. Jaffeir uses the same convenient analogy to throw all the guilt for his disasters upon his father-in-law, and perhaps also, unconsciously, to blame his wife for getting him into difficulties in the first place. The rest of the play continues to exploit the analogy so as to limit and modify the various relationships through comparison. As late as Act V we find the scene in which Belvidera softens her father's fierceness juxtaposed with that in which Aquilina draws a dagger and sends her Antonio into an amorous ecstasy: "Swear at my feet and tremble at my fury," Aquilina cries, to which Antonio, echoing the content of Priuli's

"Not one of 'em [the conspirators] but what shall be immortal," swears to save Pierre "by these dear fragrant foots and little toes, sweet as, e e e e my Nacky Nacky Nacky" (203, 114, 207–208). The parallelism and discrimination are plain. They are the culmination of a series of graded comparisons between unnatural tyranny and unnatural sex.

These two are tied together by Renault (whose lust and ambition mark him a descendent of the heroic "statesman"), by the allusions to Shaftesbury, by the Venetian ceremony of marrying Doge and sea (IV.237–238), and by the images of a sinking and burning whore with which the conspirators deride Venice, and with which senatorial tyranny ironically stains Belvidera (compare II.292–294 with V.354–362). A strain of imagery related to animals, degraded and bestial, further binds the analogies and clarifies the special and yet not tainted nature of Jaffeir's and Belvidera's love. The unnatural Priuli is a dog (I.300); Jaffeir has been degraded by tyranny to the state of a dog (II.79–83), a more perverse dog than any animal; the violence of the conspirators will make the senators die like the dogs they are (II.120–121), and thus nobly avert the same fate for themselves (III.ii.447): the full meaning of these images can only be seen in relationship to one another, but they are governed by the central dog image of the play, that related to Antonio's canine fetishism. In turn, one's evaluation of the continual erotic raptures and pastoralism of Jaffeir and Belvidera is conditioned by the context of animals and "natural" behavior— the various lamb, lion, ass, owl, serpent, worm, toad, kite images that Otway uses in similes—corrupted by Antonio in particular, and by senate and conspirators in general.[10]

These complexities of evaluation, as I have said, proceed from Jaffeir's own mixed mind, and their action on the audience is the

10. Antonio's behavior, of course, has degraded the eagle (Aquilina), the noblest of soaring creatures, to a female pudend (nick-nack). See the entry under "nick-nack" in Eric Partridge, *A Dictionary of Slang and Unconventional English* (5th ed., New York, 1961).

same as their action upon him. We too feel bruised by the moral intricacies that Otway introduces and leaves hanging, and our general receptiveness to the pathos of the play increases accordingly. One can legitimately decide that Otway is not really interested in morality at all except as a means of organizing his presentation of tragic events, states of mind, or problems of personal integrity. The subordination of moral interests to personal action, which the heroic play encouraged, has not ceased with Otway or with his contemporaries. Political interests too remain subordinate; and despite censors' pens and prologues' demagoguery, political allusions in Restoration tragedy almost never do more than add spice or set norms in an otherwise conventional and apolitical plot. If one reads Southerne's *Loyal Brother* or Settle's *Female Prelate* one finds that they are standard stuff—*The Female Prelate* largely reworks *The Empress of Morocco*, and is just as entertaining in just the same way. Lee's *Lucius Junius Brutus,* banned for its fulsome Whiggery, concentrates on no political program but on Titus' suffering. What was offensive was that Lee took Whiggery as the natural state of affairs; as the cause of the catastrophe, it is implicated along with all other political systems. Whig ideas are merely a constant mode of allusion, as it were. Similarly, the Toryism of *Venice Preserv'd* consists pretty much in its taking advantage of Shaftesbury's being out of favor, and that is by no means crucial even to the Nicky-Nacky scenes, in effect or *raison d'être.* The primary function of the politics in Restoration tragedy is to foster that pathos which the theoretical critics demanded. At this point, we return to our observations on form and content in Lee's language. Otway, despite the brilliance and coherence of *Venice Preserv'd,* can be charged with disjoining form and content, so that the organizing fact of moral dilemma becomes more significant than the nature of the dilemma, the external appeal of suffering more significant than its quality. It is perhaps best to skirt the prescriptive aesthetic judgments lurking here, but just as well to keep their contingencies in mind.

Our cursory discussion has, I hope, begun to make evident the freshness and intelligence that Lee and Banks sometimes, and Otway almost always, brought to the practice of their art within its historical context. These men shared in the development of a new and suitable diction, taking into account the cry for Nature, taking advantage of the loosening of decorum that Nature brought with her. In Lee, the effects of the heroic play found new relationships, like the pieces in a twisted kaleidoscope, save that the demands of pathos rather than those of gravity and chance brought about the specific changes. In Banks, deliberate forswearing of exotic settings, of most exotic diction (such as the rabble scene, but not the rant), and of the strikingly masculine, led to the invention of the "she-tragedy," moving toward the farthest reaches of pathos. In Otway, finally, creative use of comic techniques took advantage of relaxed decorum to root the plays in a broader kind of naturalism than one finds in either Lee or Banks, and to define the values of Restoration tragedy through a typically comic ethos in *The Orphan* and analogical comic scenes in *Venice Preserv'd*. Otway also carries to its psychological extreme the elements of passivity and introversion that the pathetic play involves, so that his tragedies take on symbolic shape dependent not on the rules of the genre but at least partially on the hero's consciousness elevated into law. Presumably, his later tragedies would have followed along these lines; he would have investigated more and more deeply the potentialities of the form. As it is, the end of his development effectually coincided with the end of the historical development of seventeenth-century tragedy. Not until Rowe were the lines of evolution from Otway gathered up into a new and significant kind of tragedy. In the meanwhile, tragedians profited as they could from the technical accomplishments that they had been bequeathed. They wrote plays that were often thin, repetitious, and superficially embellished; occasionally, they wrote the eloquent tragedy that was inherent in their legacy.

III

THE GENRE: TASTES AND TECHNIQUES

7

ETHOS

TO DEFINE A GENRE SOLELY IN TERMS DEDUCED FROM EFFECTS upon an audience—and, as I have tried to show, that is what later Restoration tragedy did—produces works whose parts are clearly differentiated in action (to avoid boredom) but inter-changeable in function. Like the petals of a tulip, they grow from and point toward a single center. In Chapters 3 through 6, I discussed the changes in the center and the new kinds of unity that those changes instituted. In the final chapters, I should like to expand on some of those observations, treated analytically; the "interchangeable function" of the parts will be taken for granted. To a large extent, these divisions are merely a matter of conven-ience: one cannot talk about historical development without describing that which developed, nor can one describe intelli-gently without reference to historical context. With the material included in the present part, I have been equally ruthless, coarsely chopping it into three sections, labeled "Ethos," "Struc-ture," and "Language," more as a simple means of talking about the genre than as a necessary or natural way of dividing it. From these three discussions, we may emerge, I hope, with a fuller recognition of the ways in which the tragedies operate.

Nothing is more noticeable in the plays than their incessant reference to pastoral, and it is there that a consideration of their ethos should begin. In Chapter 5 I have touched upon pastoral as an ideal of private life, an implicit daydream for a hero and heroine caught in implacable events. In fact, pastoral was always implicit in the heroic, as its overt development in the late heroic play suggests that it must have been.[1] The positive values that the heroic sets up and defines imply the various negations of those values—otherwise to set up values is a tautology—and, in practice, the heroic play thrives on those negations. The amorphous feelings of the audience toward community and self-assertion are meant to be refined by love and honor, while, dramatically, the playwrights have used the same feelings as grounds for salaciousness and violence. The villains, in turn, share ends with the hero and heroine—the audience has no defined "ends" for its feelings—but pervert the proper motives to those of lust and ambition. Pastoral, as a third possibility, denies the heroic process, to which the villains by and large adhere, and relies upon its own kind of happy conclusion, which is psychologically analogous to that of the heroic play. Each of these three patterns of value, the audience's, the villain's, the pastoral man's, gives the English heroic play a body and breadth of implication different from that of its French or Caroline counterparts. In this heroic scheme, pastoral values had thrived largely among the ladies, who had been more tenderly loving, timorous, and domestic than heroes. Later, however, after tragedy had chosen to live *muliebriter,* heroes too accepted rural retirement and the apotheosis of love. When Almira, in Henry Smith's *The Princess of Parma* (1699), invites Doria to join her beneath "a fragrant Shade of twisted Greens, / The peaceful seat of Sacred Innocence," where the senses can be delighted with arbors, meads, streams, and birds, and where "No wish of Honour shall our rest devour," Doria can reply honestly for a great bevy of his fellow

1. Hallett Smith remarks that "heroic and pastoral always imply each other, for one is in a sense the obverse of the other. The great nexus in which they meet is the question of ambition."—*Elizabethan Poetry* (Cambridge, Mass., 1952), p. 323. The observation is particularly appropriate to pastoral in the Restoration drama; for unlike Renaissance pastoral, which often presented the rural scene as a microcosm of the great world (Sidney's *Arcadia,* for example), the ideal pastoral of the Restoration hero offered stasis. The personal achievement, the verbal ebullience, the visual grandeur, and the continuous self-fulfillment of the heroic world are all cut short.

tragic heroes, "There could I fix my Happiness forever" (C3ᵛ; Act II).

The pastoral is not, of course, merely a way of making tragedy womanish. It grows within the fixed contexts of the genre almost mechanically, as the steam slowly leaks from heroism, and deflation in one part causes commensurate swelling in another. As in Lee, sensationalism grows with it; or, as in Banks, villainy. The elements of tragedy readjust themselves to make up for the loss of extravagance, of powerful characterization, of an attainable ideal. In these terms, pastoral has two functions. One is to present a counterpoise to dismal actualities, a psychological possibility of vacationing forever from corrupt courts, the contests of ambition, the dangers of martial glory, the deceitful lures of fortune. This counterpoise depends on the play's accepting love as the supreme value, so that the idyllic state will not be grossly wanting; that, as we have seen, the playwrights were quite ready to do. For the characters, then, pastoral represents a psychological nostrum that cures, or dissolves, the difficulties that the plays' painful reality forces upon them. It devalues that reality and insists upon another, often connected with that great goddess of the Augustans, Nature.

In this way, the alterations of value that are characteristic of all pastoral redefine the characters' goals, and therefore their plights. Pastoral can, quite obviously, answer problems raised by the sudden disgrace of a conquering hero, which is a standard Restoration turn of plot. Pastoral is the answer to political conflict. Mrs. Pix's Queen Catharine is happier powerless and united with Tudor than as a potentate: Isabella glosses this to prove "Possessing the dear object that's beloved, / Superiour to ambition, a sublimer Joy," and asks only to live in a cottage and "humble / Vineyard" with her Clarence, to "taste balmy slumbers, which the / Busie Statesman, and the fair false one / Never knows" (E4; Act IV). It resolves love-honor agonies. Agamemnon (*Heroick Love*) promises to make himself "A Shepherd, or an humble Villager" if he can have Chruseis, and he denounces heroes as "Lunaticks mis-call'd / That cheat themselves, and part with all that's precious / For Toys and Gew Gawes" (K3ʳ; Act V). Nothing could be more natural for the characters than this resort to seclusion, and nothing more useful for the tragedian than this means of making reality more pathetic by posing it against its opposite.

Within these Restoration plays, the usurpation of the heroic ideal by its pastoral antithesis produces a particular emphasis on the self-sufficiency of the pastoral condition. One can see this clearly, for instance, in Banks' *Cyrus the Great* (1696). Croesus, the sage in Banks as in Herodotus, speaks what might have been a boast in the earlier drama, describing his mind soaring above his fortune, and concludes, "Yet in / Despite of all thou canst, I'm *Croesus* still." It is not, however, a boast. The chastening experience of defeat has forced him to recognize his own strength and the instability of this world; his refuge, or discovery, is couched in the terms of pastoral. The happiest man, Solon has told him, is one of

> . . . no mean nor mighty Fortune;
> His Wife not fair, nor homely, but belov'd,
> And virtuous, and his Children all obedient,
> Who, like the first Man, liv'd in paradice,
> And never press'd the Strangers luscious Fruits,
> Nor drank but what his own full Vines did yield;
> Fed on the Flesh of his own teeming Flocks,
> And wore no Cloaths but what their Backs afforded;
> In his Pale grew all his sustenance,
> And in his Bosom all the World's content.   (C2ʳ; Act II)

The analogy between the autonomy and eventual calm of heroic and pastoral heroes could hardly be clearer. It is accentuated by Banks' having taken his image of retirement not from the peasantry—a social antithesis to the heroic world—but from the classics. Classical influence works specifically in terms of narrative sources like Herodotus, Plutarch, and Aulus Gellius. Still more significantly, it works in terms of norm: Banks' Croesus comes from Horace's epodes and Claudian's man of Verona, so that the social ideal can directly challenge the heroic. And inasmuch as *Cyrus the Great* ends with four major characters dead—one of them mad, another hugging the lacerated pieces of her lover's body like Theseus at the end of Seneca's *Hippolytus*—the challenge is carried through.

I spoke above of two functions for the pastoral, and have discussed the first, pastoral as an ideal within the context of the play. The other depends secondarily on pastoral itself, primarily on its corollaries, such as love, peace, superiority to fortune, and removal of competition. These are involved in any providential scheme; and although theology does not set its mark in any real way upon these tragedies, the playwright at times chooses to provide some sort of poetic justice, which openly imposes the order of nature upon an unnatural and disordered dramatic world, leveling hierarchies and negating all heroic efforts. Dramatic madness, for example, is thus providential. Heroines, in a kind of mental retirement from distress, see themselves united with their beloveds; villains find that their worldly craft has been worthless. Or, occasionally, providence of this sort manifests itself in a vision such as that at the end of Crowne's *Darius*, when the ghost of the sentimental king appears "*brightly habited*" over his murderers' bodies. Or, finally, we may end with a dose of Christianity, as in Powell's [?] *The Fatal Discovery* (1698), where Cornaro sleeps with both his mother and (eighteen years later) his half-sister/daughter, without knowing their relationships to him: "Let no one censure poor *Cornaro*'s Fate," advises the concluding quatrain of the play,

> But think it hard, he was Unfortunate:
> Tho' Virtue here han't met its due Regard,
> There is a place where it must have Reward.

I would argue that these endings are made far more acceptable because the genre in which they appear admits pastoral within it. If Restoration tragedy admitted theology to its world, such endings might be taken as an enlargement of the principles of reality presented in the first four acts of a play. But the very nature of affective drama and of serial construction runs counter to what I have called "fabulist" construction, and therefore to dramatic forms that mirror Providence. Rewards and punishments imposed by poetic justice negate, rather than metaphysically amplify, the system of values that the action has implied. For this reason, playwrights do well to include a continuing system of "negative" values in their tragedies, so that the shifting of gears at the end may be less harsh and more satisfying. Pastoral, as such a system of "negative" values, serves admirably. By denying the world as presented, it makes possible a more thoroughgoing denial of that world at the end of the play.

Whether as a formal and psychological element or as an enabling clause for a providential ending, pastoral attains immense importance in late Restoration tragedy. It can do so in large part because it follows from a certain complex of assumptions that dominated the serious drama before the eighties, a complex that one can roughly denote as "Epicureanism."[2] At times, it is true, the lineage becomes hard to trace: the heroic play can be called "Epicurean" only if that term remains loosely defined, as indeed it remained loosely defined in the Restoration itself. None the less, we have testimony that at least for polemic purposes the heroic hero found himself lumped with libertines, Hobbesians, and Epicureans.[3] The self-sufficiency of the hero and the Epicurean again links them; and, if it be objected that the hero thrives on action, the Epicurean on repose, it should be recalled that the destiny promised the heroic hero

2. My discussion has been influenced by Maren-Sofie Røstvig, *The Happy Man. Studies in the Metamorphoses of a Classical Ideal*, Vol. I, 1600–1700 (revised ed., New York, 1962), especially pp. 227–310. For general documentation about Restoration Epicureanism, see Thomas Franklin Mayo, *Epicurus in England 1650–1725* (n.p., [1934]).

3. Kirsch, *Dryden's Heroic Drama*, pp. 35–46.

is not more warfare but more peace, not more striving but more
fixity, not more love-pangs but more love. Whatever else may
be necessary and virtuous for him in order to prove his individual worth, his hopes take their image from Eden. Moreover,
the similarity of attitude in the heroic play and the Etheregean
comedy suggests the essential hedonism, however strongly tem-
pered by social pressures, that motivates a Maximin (quite
openly) or an Almanzor. Nor ought one to forget the audience,
whose hedonism feasted safely on a glut of feeling in both
heroic and pathetic plays, like different courses from the same
kitchen. In short, the Epicureanism of the pastoral, which I
shall discuss, comes logically from the "Epicureanism" of the
heroic. It should be seen as part of a continuing ethos in one
respect, at the same time as it breaks with the heroic ethos in
another.

Here we should look at the components of Epicurean pastoralism. One, already mentioned, is the self-sufficiency of the
protagonist, a quality stressed by a number of classical philoso-
phies among which there is no point for us in distinguishing.
The ancients, including Cicero and St. Augustine, did not
always make such distinctions either. As Gataker protested,
". . . to bring *Pleasure* and *Discipline* into a Competition,
this looks like a very unhandsome and unreasonable Fancy. For
all that, some have been so hardy as to endeavour the Recon-
ciling these Contradictions; and to make the Matter the more
Extraordinary, it has been attempted by some of the *Stoicks*."
He goes on to cite Seneca's reconciliation of these "Contradictions," protesting in disagreement that "in *Morality* 'tis the *End*
which gives the *Form* and Distinction to an Action: And here
we shall find the *Stoick* and *Epicurean Philosophers* differ . . ."[4] Gataker's objection bears no relevance to Restoration

4. Gataker's "Discourse" appears in *The Emperor Marcus Antoninus His
Conversation With Himself*, trans. Jeremy Collier (2nd ed., corrected, Lon-
don, 1708), p. 7. See also Temple's essay "Upon the Gardens of Epicurus," in
The Works of Sir William Temple, 2 vols. [ed. Jonathan Swift] (London,

tragedy, however, in which the only characters who are pastoral Epicureans are the oppressed and virtuous. Whatever outward manifestations tally with the expected Epicureanism can thereby be put into the same set of feelings and responses; Croesus' speech quoted above, for instance, fits within our capacious Epicureanism by accommodation with the prevailing categories that the audiences had learned to use in dealing with stage ideas. In the same way, Dryden's Cleomenes fits within these conventions:

> Dejected! no, it never shall be said,
> That Fate had power upon a Spartan Soul:
> My mind upon its own Centre stands unmov'd,
> And Stable; as the Fabrick of the World:
> Propt on it self; still I am *Cleomenes*: . . .
>
> (B; Act I)

One may call this Spartan rigor, Stoicism, *sapientia et fortitudo*, stale morsels of heroic play, as one likes; but if one does so, he should not be surprised to find the same Cleomenes later turning to his wife to say:

> *Cleora!* Thou and I, as Lovers should,
> Will hand in hand to the dark Mansions go,
> Where Life no more can cheat us into Woe;
> That sucking in each others latest Breath,
> We may transfuse our Souls, and put the change on Death.
>
> (H^v; Act IV)

Nor should he be surprised to find that the beloved Cleora does not appear in Plutarch, Dryden's source. After all, Dryden had shortly before dedicated his *Don Sebastian* to the Earl of Leicester as a "second *Atticus*"—the first having been an Epicurean—and there announced that "the ruggedness of a *Stoic* is only a silly affectation of being a god."

The reason that the classical ideal of self-sufficiency becomes

---

1720), I, 173: ". . . the Difference between [Stoics and Epicureans] seems not easily discovered."

part of stage Epicureanism is simply that the plays are dominated by love, a refined hedonism. Therefore, as Dennis charged
in attacking *Cato*, "a Nest of *Stoicks* [can] supply us, with no
more proper Persons for an excellent Tragedy, than a Nest of
Fools can do for an excellent Comedy."[5] Stoics repress the passions that tragedy demands they show. Other classical philoso-
phies too had their faults. Aristotelian magnanimity had long
been part of a heroic ideal that the pathetic play was rejecting;
Platonism suffered the double taint of mysticism, incomprehen-
sible on the stage even if it had been congenial to the playwright, and spiritualization of love. From all these difficulties
Epicureanism was free, and to it most if not all of the classical
strain through these tragedies can be referred. As to contemporary associations with isolation from society, those too can be
called "Epicurean." Even the casual reader of Restoration verse
will need no proof for this assertion, for these associations take
specific shape from the amorous pastoral lyric, which enters
Restoration tragedy directly in songs and indirectly in clear
thematic parallelism with the ideal of retirement and love that
we have been discussing.

We touch here upon a congeries of ideas beyond the scope of
this book to examine. One can, however, surely perceive the
connections between classical simplicity (reason, Golden Age),
simplicity of style (natural style), and simplicity of pastoral life:
the hero and heroine of pathetic tragedy committed themselves
to all. M.-S. Røstvig amplifies these connections in talking of
the *"beatus vir* as innocent Epicurean": "If reason is inherent
in all men and the equal inheritance of all, a reversion to a state
of nature becomes tantamount to a revival of the reign of reason, and the Golden Age (or state of innocence) becomes the
age in which blind and destructive passions as yet had not upset
the original mental and emotional balance of men. Mrs. Behn
interpreted this reign of reason as a state in which the noble

5. *Critical Works of John Dennis,* II, 54.

passion of love was unhampered by false conceptions of honour, dignity, or worth, and so to the classical denunciation of ambition she added her own of false honour and modesty."[6] The world, the arena for heroic action, is essentially unreasonable, not only in its corruption but also in its norms and criteria. If we think back to the criticisms of the rhymed play, we can see that the union of nature and reason that the critics demanded now appears concurrent with the union of nature and reason that disavows the content of the heroic play as well as its style.

We are led to an important stylistic point. In the heroic play, "reason" and "nature" essentially refer to the genre and its procedures, as Dryden pointed out to Howard. The criterion of "reason," applied to language, means the rationalizing of feeling into artful patterns, while "nature," as something to be imitated, is established by the rules of the genre. Like the heroic character, the heroic genre is self-sufficient. The pathetic play, however, refers reason and reasonableness, nature and the natural, to life outside the play itself. It gives up its self-sufficiency just as its hero, through marital and social ties and through oppression, has had to surrender his. In other words, we can see close resemblances between the ways in which playwrights and heroes, in both heroic and pathetic plays, conduct themselves. The self-containment of the heroic play mirrors that of the heroic hero; the natural mimesis of the pathetic play mirrors its hero's social accommodation. We are led to ask whether we can go further and find in the structure of the pathetic play itself some analogue to Epicurean pastoral, which restores to the pathetic hero a measure of self-sufficiency by placing him imaginatively within a protective context of reason and nature, by making his social ties the fulfillments of desire instead of the sources of peril. In short, we should find the plays striving to establish some sort of reasonable and natural relationship with.

6. Røstvig, *The Happy Man*, I, 283.

an outside world, so that they, like their heroes, can regain their lost freedom from contingency.

In one sense, the normal mimetic relationship that the play bears to outside life restores this freedom, provides "a protective context of reason and nature." If the play is good—and all plays must assume that they are—its very interest in fidelity to life becomes its justification. For reasons that we can approach by way of stylistics, then, as well as by way of affective interests, the pathetic play should commit itself to more and more accurate imitation of life. In part it does, of course, and probably would have done so without those sociological prods of middle-class influence on which many critics place great importance. But these relationships established by normal mimesis do not maintain an exact parallel with the hero's Epicurean pastoralism, which is made necessary, after all, because his normal relationships have broken down. We should still find some imaginative means by which the play shapes the life outside it so as to make a haven for itself and its ideals. Overt didacticism is such a means, and the tragedies' readiness to embrace didacticism must be accounted for in some measure on such stylistic grounds as I have been suggesting. So must the pathetic play's affective technique: while the heroic play does not try to induce feelings of love and honor in the audience, the pathetic play does try to induce love and its sister pity, and to make the feelings of the audience the eventual and essential refuge for its virtuous characters. The nature, reason, respect for feeling, and simplicity that the spectacle of tragedy brings to the society in the audience serves to redeem the evils committed by society and its standards within the play. The imagination of the protagonists creates an Epicurean pastoral ideal; the imagination of the playwright makes that ideal a reality within the hearts of the audience.

In developing these stylistic implications, I have digressed from the Epicurean pastoral itself. I should like now to return to it, and to discuss the advantages of labeling this complex of attitudes "Epicurean" besides the two already mentioned, i.e., the linkage with seemingly different attitudes in earlier plays, heroic and comic, and the support given to pastoral through seemingly unrelated references to classical fortitude and self-sufficiency. A third, minor, advantage is that one can appreciate the significance of the repeated atomic imagery in the tragedies, which may be understood as one more testimony "to the effect that Epicurus had indeed risen from the dead, and that the atomistic theory had burst its seams."[7] Banks' villainous Northumberland and pathetic Mary speak of "justling Atoms" and "disjoynted Atoms" respectively as having formed the world (*Innocent Usurper*, C2; Act II. *Island Queens*, H2; Act IV). "Revelling Atoms made the Universe," says Phraartes in Crowne's late heroic *Destruction of Jerusalem* (E2ᵛ; Act III). Francis Fane's Axalla in *The Sacrifice* (I3; Act V), asks that the earth be shaken "To Shreds, to Atoms, to a Second Chaos." There are many more instances of language such as this, taken from the vocabulary of a revived Epicureanism, which imply an interest in or acquaintance with a material cosmogony to match the tragedies' vested interest in a love both physical and orderly placed in a natural setting both physical and orderly.

More important, I think, is our ability to use the linking of doctrines in a philosophic system, like Epicureanism, to illuminate the linking of seemingly disparate themes in unsystematic art. Epicurus' pastoral depends directly upon the exercise of the imaginative will, as does the pastoral in pathetic plays; both have a specific insistence on the freedom of that will, a freedom often obscured by the impotence and victimization that pathetic drama entails. Epicurus writes:

> . . . I take for granted that there is in us a free or arbitrary power of reason, that is, a faculty elective and productive of that which reason hath judged good, and of avoiding and

7. Edward Niles Hooker, "Dryden and the Atoms of Epicurus," *ELH*, XXIV (1957), 186.

shunning what it hath judged ill . . . True indeed it is,
that in things void of reason, some effects are necessary,
. . . but, in Man, endu'd with reason, and as far as he
makes use of that reason, there can be no Necessity. Hence
it was, we endeavoured to assert the declination of motions
in Atoms, that we might from thence deduce, how Fortune might sometimes intervene, and put in for a share
amongst human affairs, yet, that which is in us, our Will
not be destroy'd.

It behoves us to employ all our wit and endeavours to
maintain our own free-will against that sempiternal motion,
and not to suffer wickedness to escape unculpable.[8]

The condition that this passage describes is one of worldly time
or duration ruled by necessities (I use the plural to suggest the
nominalism that an atomic theory implies) with what one might
call a proconsular status. They have *de facto* power, but may
be constantly overthrown by a constant series of acts of human
will. Their duration, their self-perpetuation, can be countered
by a man's renewal of himself through acts of will. Epicurus'
"wickedness" and "culpable" indicate moreover that he here
sees will and self morally. But Epicurus also proposes an amoral
and (in terms of duration and necessity) static world of pastoral
retreat, symbolized by the garden. This second world, half real
and half a state of mind, magically transcends the "sempiternal
motion" of necessities. To enter it, morality is a precondition;
after entrance, morality and will are sloughed by the self,
which exists hedonically, its motion and rest, its delight and
serenity, now taking place in a newly created and newly defined
sort of time.

No other description, I think, better suits the relationships
between the individual and his environment, free will and

8. I am using the version of Epicurus' philosophy most familiar to the
Restoration, that found in Thomas Stanley, *The History of Philosophy*. This
passage comes from the third edition (London, 1701), Part XIII, chap. vi,
p. 610.

necessity, imagination and reason, that Restoration tragedy offers us.[9] Here I am once more speaking of the genre, not of every isolated play. Some of the plays may treat these relationships differently. Their reasons for doing so may be aesthetic, ideological, or related to the author's ineptitudes. None of these reasons can be appreciated, however, without a sense of what the common conventions of the tragedies were. Generally, then, environment becomes almost identified with necessity: since Restoration tragedy usually avoids analysis of motives, or even complex presentation of motives, the villains strike upon the hero's world with the force of unreasonable fate. The *clinamina* of their vices appear as arbitrary as those of atoms. Within the pathetic play, furthermore, our sense of arbitrariness increases for two reasons. One is that these tragedies focus on the suffering of the hero, so that the villains inherit a particularly causal function. The other is that, as we saw in considering *Venice Preserv'd*, events in these plays may be distorted to render them from the hero's point of view; this still further flattens the villains into phenomena, not people or exemplars. In other words, they cannot benefit from the objectivity provided by psychology in a modern novel or by norms of virtue in most Renaissance and heroic plays. One does find numbers of villains as absolute, and as much the scourges of God, as was the Tudor Vice: Dampierre in Edward Filmer's *The Unnatural Brother*, for instance, laughs at his villainies, at penitents, at dead lovers, at his own tortures, and so on. But even a sulky king has the same simple black effect as a Dampierre; and so, differences between villains are merely formal, offering various means of resolving the tragedy but not various means of resolving whatever cognitive problems the tragedy has set up. As we move toward blocking characters who are less and less culpable, like Lucius Junius Brutus or Zara (*The Mourning Bride*), the

9. The relation of time and will in Restoration tragedy may be compared with that in Corneille and Racine, as they are rather orphically discussed by Georges Poulet, *Studies in Human Time* (New York, 1959), pp. 105–130.

use of the blocking character as an arm of arbitrary fate grows clearer still.

The hero, of course, is sinless, or sins accidentally, like Cornaro (*The Fatal Discovery*) or Don Sebastian in Dryden's play, both of whom are trapped by fate into incest. Except for Otway, Lee, and Mrs. Trotter, there is no tragedian, I should say, who shows any particular predilection for confronting a weak hero with a moral dilemma. Choice, however, is not abridged so sharply by genre as in the heroic play. The more the hero and heroine invite empathy the more one believes in their personalities and so, in their free will. Their very suffering thereby leads to the illusion that they are real people and might be capable of acting otherwise. Within the reality of the dramatic world, this attributed free will works in moral terms; while translated into human imagination, its terms are amoral (or post-moral) and pastoral, as in Epicurus. Epicurus, the pragmatist, redeems imagination by passing it off as part of a practical recipe for happiness, as the result of choice. Restoration tragedy does the same thing, marking the hero's wisdom and virtue by the same imaginative choice that would free him from the need for either. The divorce that the pathetic play introduces between external and mental acts, which the heroic play kept in the same harness, comes to its paradoxical result here. Heroes who suffer outwardly act mentally, thereby freeing themselves for mental passivity (the delights of love without care or will) and physical (erotic) acts. In the real world, as I have said, their only guaranteed freedom comes from the love and pity of those agents of theatrical providence, the audience.

So far, my discussion has stressed pastoral and Epicureanism because they are present in themselves and also show the coherence of much else that might seem shallow or incoherent. We may now turn to a related matter, the portrayal of and allegiances of the hero and heroine. In considering this historically, the importance of perspective scenery should not be neglected, since it provides the visual context for the metaphor of "portrayal" as well as a spatial localization that parallels localization of duty or feeling. Such scenery, of course, seldom appeared even in the private houses, like Blackfriars or Salisbury Court, before the Restoration; against scattered references to scenery and backdrops in these houses, usually for plays that had been put on with scenery at court, we have the word of the *Historia Histrionica:* "The Plays and Actors, of the last Age, . . . cou'd support themselves meerly from their own Merit; the weight of the Matter, and goodness of the Action, without Scenes and Machines."[10] In these private houses, as before in the Globe and its fellow theatres, fluidity of setting and action complemented tragedies in which heroes defined themselves, characterized themselves, created for the audience a self susceptible of definition and characterization. "Scenes and Machines," however, complemented masques and court plays in which no such definition took place; in fact, where allegorical schemes and dialectic conventions made it unneeded. Nor was this radically changed after the Restoration and the general introduction of illusionistic scenery. In fact, as the heroic play developed, such scenery became integral with it, not only to give some gloss of verisimilitude to exotic speech and action, but also to express the heroic ethos in visual terms.[11]

A delightful example of this may be found in Francis Fane's unacted and anachronistic *The Sacrifice* (1686), which includes *"an Amphitheatre of Crown'd Mummies"* (C2), *"flashes of Lightning and Smoak"* (C3ʳ), *"Thunder, Lightning, Rainbows inverted, a bloody Arm, Comet, &c."* (F4ʳ), and *"Mount Atlas, with a Face and Beard like a Man made by Trees, which sinks down by degrees with soft Music; and at the top of him appear Angels with flaming Swords"* (H4). This sort of dis-

---

10. Quoted in G. E. Bentley, *The Jacobean and Caroline Stage,* II (Oxford, 1941), 693–694. For various references to scenery in the theatre, see Bentley's index to volumes I and II, under "Theatre, Scenery in" (II, 744).

11. No one was more keenly aware of the integral importance of scenery in the heroic play than Dryden. See Ker, I, 154–155.

play is the scenic equivalent of the action at the beginning of the play; there, after proxies for the emperors of Greece, Persia, China, and Russia have kissed Tamburlaine's footstool, the Master of Ceremonies announces:

> *Mr. Cer.* Two and Twenty *African* Kings beg admission.
> [22 *Kings appear*
> *Tam.* Let the Kings wait till the Afternoon.

Unfortunately, the rest of Fane's play is not much good; or, rather, fortunately, for the merit of the play does not obscure for us the elements of technique that Fane had imitated from heroic dramatists. We can understand that just as rant categorized the heroic hero—to adhere to the distinction made in Chapter 4—so did spectacle. Both had specific theatric functions. And just as opera in the later Restoration took over the elements of rant, changing them into musical intonation and vocal agility, opera took over spectacle.

The pathetic play, in respect to definition of character, thus found itself with a useless past. Nor could it have used spectacle in any event. Within the absolute vistas of perspective scenery, the heroic hero had behaved absolutely, becoming "the personification of the better qualities which society wants to find in its members."[12] As honor, that public quality, coincided with private gratification, and as love, that most private of feelings, turned out to locate the hero within social patterns, so the heroic hero assumed the external visual splendor like a mantle and, in turn, acted only in the modes that it made permissible. None of this helps the pathetic playwright. Cut off by time and theatrical practice from the questioning of identity on the Shakespearean stage, by ideology and theatrical practice from the categorization of identity on the heroic stage, he had

---

12. Selma Assir Zebouni, *Dryden: A Study in Heroic Characterization* (Baton Rouge, La., 1965), p. 93. Although Zebouni's book seems to me largely untrustworthy, it analyzes well the absolutism of the standards for a hero's conduct.

to find whatever means he could or abandon altogether the defining of his protagonist.

By and large, playwrights abandoned any notions of substantive identity. However vivid the hero may be, he remains a stock character; perhaps a fortiori, so do all the other characters. He has no significant past, except perhaps in Otway. He embodies no complex moral development. His present must be extremely confined by the confined subject matter of the plays and range of action possible to a thwarted and innocent hero. As we have seen in analyzing Titus' opening speech in *Lucius Junius Brutus* or Chamont's dream in *The Orphan,* his experiences refer not to him as a unique man, but to the situations in which he, as a generalized or representative character, finds himself. When one speaks of "his" imagination or perceptions, one commonly means more to localize a point of view than to attribute it. "His" subjectivity becomes objectified in Lee and Otway partly because the hero only fitfully shows enough individuality to support a subjective life of his own. Eventually, to most modern readers, the hero is a bore.

On the Restoration stage, he was not a bore because he had sympathetic appeal, due in part to his "natural" idiom and in part to Messrs. Betterton, Verbruggen, and Smith. Some may not consider these as literary reasons, and view the playwright's ability to hide behind his actors as a fatal convenience. At times it was, but it was also a *passe partout,* allowing a certain illusion to be maintained, a certain suspension of thought to be induced, so that the author could pass on to matters he could more simply and profitably handle on the stage. Exclusion of the past and narrow focus on the present enabled him to depict the continuousness and terror of oppressive fate, and to throw a bright accent on the imaginative and virtuous orders that we have already discussed. In the repeated imagery of pastoral ease, one can detect the verbal and mental projection of the very scenic support that development of the stage had denied to pathetic plays. The classical firmness and duty that mark Augus-

tanism in England found representation in numbers of plays—
*Cleomenes, Regulus, Pausanias, The Roman Bride's Revenge,
The Fate of Capua, Pyrrhus, Caligula* all date from the last
decade of the seventeenth century—which necessarily depend
on non-introspective protagonists. Here too one can detect a
restoration, through the classical historians and the classical
ideal, of the absolute standards inherent in heroics; the self is
defined only functionally in these tragedies. Precisely for that
reason, they could act as models of *pietas* for the age of William
III, with its special demands upon the political conscience.

This *pietas* fits with the kind of egalitarianism that makes
itself evident in the lowering of the hero to the level of empathy
and pathos. One can even make facile connections with the
gentilities of the periodical essayists and with the social breadth
shown in Farquhar's comedies. In any event, it is certain that
the hero finds himself not only socially tied to, but also considered socially equal with, the other principals of the play.
Physically, he can appear, like Hormidas in Settle's *Distress'd
Innocence,* "in a Post so vile, doom'd ev'n to water / The very
Camels of the Army," "Naked to th'Waste, his galling Feet all
bare; / His tender Flesh parcht with the scorching Sun" (D4;
Act III). Much more important is that the kind of loyalty expected of him is the kind expected of any subject, any husband
or father; this objective application of norms through the politics
of public and private life is what may remind one of Addison
and Farquhar. The sexes are leveled, too. The heroic play
presented a masculine world, as Etherege and Wycherley had,
in which women were valued for chastity, fidelity, and beauty.
Pathetic tragedy gives women more independent humanity
through a new depth of feeling, and transfers chastity and fidelity (if not beauty) to men as well.

At the same time, all conduct in these plays proceeds from an
ethical rather than a religious or egotistic basis. Regicide, for
example, seems scandalous for metaphysical reasons (real or
jerrybuilt) in *The Maid's Tragedy,* for reasons of *gloire* in

Boyle's *Tryphon,* but for reasons of nature in Cibber's *Xerxes.*
Aranthes in that play declares:

> . . . When Subjects
> Are no more the Care of Kings, we then
> Have only left the Laws of Nature to Protect us,
> And Nature tyes us all to Self Defence.   (D2; Act II)

Although Cibber wants to present this reasoning as rash, his
concluding moral statement, in the mouth of Mardonius, does
not renege on its implications:

> Let Kings and jarring Subjects hence be warn'd,
> Not to oppress, or drive Revenge too far:
> Kings are but Men, and Men by Nature err;
> Subjects are Men, and cannot always bear.
> Much shou'd be born before Revenge is sought:
> Ever Revenge on Kings is dearly bought.   (G4ᵛ; Act V)

Reason and nature join to form the system of ethical values in
the pathetic play, as they join to form its system of Epicurean
pastoral. Once more, in the submission of kings to the rule of
reason, the egalitarianism of which we were just speaking reappears. Here, quite clearly, we can also see that the functional
definition of characters' identities, not anything more personal,
determines the *pietas* for each.

One curious sidelight of the joint rule of reason and duty involves the virginity of the heroine. For largely economic causes,
society was placing an ever-increasing value on virginity.[13] As
models of *pietas,* unmarried heroines had to be virgins. Yet in
reason, widows and conceivably victims of rape should have
been able to marry. Almahide was a widow, after all. The
pathetic playwrights solved the potential dilemma by treating
heroines who were not virgins like heroines who were, but by
making sure that the tragedy did not end happily. Mrs. Manley's

13. For a thorough discussion of the economic importance of virginity, see
Christopher Hill, "Clarissa Harlowe and her Times," *Essays in Criticism,* V
(1955), 315–340.

The Royal Mischief (1696), Mrs. Pix's *Queen Catharine* (1698), Southerne's *The Fate of Capua* (1700), and Jane Wiseman's *Antiochus the Great* (1702) all doom their heroes and heroines not through any inexorability of the plot but through the girls' having in each case married sometime before. The only play, I believe, in which a once-married heroine ends up happily married to the hero is Mrs. Pix's *The Czar of Muscovy* (1701). In this tragedy, Mrs. Pix ingeniously saves Marina by killing off her sinister husband, Demetrius, between ceremony and consummation. Few other tragedies, as one can see, could follow Mrs. Pix's example. For them, as for the many tragedies in which there is a rape, physical violation leads only to physical death or seclusion. Spiritual innocence finds its reward only in the imagined simplicity of pastoral or in the emotional redemption by the audience which comes from suffering and death.

All the discussion above makes it plain that the pathetic dramatists were not breaking from the characteristic subject matter of the Restoration stage. Whether they agreed overtly or not, most of the playwrights would have subscribed to the claim, in the prologue to Higgons' *The Generous Conquerour* (1702), that "generous Wits, have . . . Heroick Views, / And Love and Honour, are the Theams they chuse." The characters make no attempt to phrase their feelings in terms other than those traditional in the Restoration drama. Rheusanes (*The Injur'd Lovers*) accuses Ghinotto of having murdered his "Love and Honour" (G^v; Act IV). Helenus tells Aristeon in Hopkins' *Pyrrhus* (1695) that "Glory and Love makes us eternal foes" (D4; Act III). The very title of Granville's *Heroick Love* (1698) will indicate its contents, and although Agamemnon's tears, swooning, and loss of his lady are purely pathetic, his plight in many ways harks back to his predecessors': "Love, Piety, and Honour pull at once / All several ways—Nor know I which to follow" (C4^v; Act I). It was during the late Restoration that John Dennis wrote his *Rinaldo and Armida*

(1699), which is perhaps the most concentrated treatment of what intellectual content there is in love and honor, prefaced by a discussion of the ethics and varying thematic ambages inherent in their conflict. Even villains voice concern in these terms: Lamira, in Mrs. Trotter's *The Fatal Friendship* (1698), speaks of love and honor as ". . . the nicest, dearest parts of me" (B4; Act I); or the wicked Emperor in Walker's *Victorious Love* (1698) has a love-honor debate, rejecting any countermand to Love's "Tyrant [']s Voice" (D; Act II).

None the less, our discussion has made clear that love and honor in these plays differ in at least three important ways from those themes in heroics. First, the pathetic play follows Banks and Otway in redefining honor as duty or loyalty, what I have called *pietas*. Secondly, it treats love and honor as traits of the characters, to be attained in many possible ways, while the heroic play treats characters against a fixed grid of love and honor. As a corollary, pathetic tragedy gives the characters an imaginative, even poetic, faculty that heroic heroes do not have. Lastly, love and honor become universal commands rather than the marks of heroism; as benevolence and good faith they are part of a general social message that speaks to the ethical conscience of the audience and that offers the plays themselves an ethical basis that they had earlier lacked.

8

CONVENTIONS OF
STRUCTURE

DESCRIPTIONS OF THE TYPICAL STRUCTURES OF PLAYS TEND TO
be rather dispiriting. What might be poignant or grave in context lies flat on the critic's page, a cliché amid a school of its
equally fished-out fellows. To find a least common denominator
for the drama of artists and hacks reduces everything to tedious
naïveté or sleazy cynicism. It is for these reasons that I have
discussed the ethos of the plays first, so that the conventions of
plot may be seen tinged with artistic possibility. What then
happens, happens because of the clumsy cobbling of a Mrs.
Pix, the adeptness of a William Mountfort, or the energetic
fineness of a Dryden. It is only with the bungling author that
Restoration tragedy becomes a mere series of graduated *coups
de théâtre*, with the nature of the coups prescribed by type-
casting and sensationalism. The hack could make only the
simplest appeal to the passions, of which there are, after all,
very few: faced with the almost infinite stupidity of human
emotion, he resorted to repetition, cliché, and padding. *The
Mourning Bride* deals with the same type-casting and sensationalism, the same appeals to the passions, and it must be seen
in terms of that context. To realize this, however, is not to
insist on the priority of that context in the mind of a Congreve
or in one's criticism of his accomplishment. What matters is his
conversion of artistic hazard into triumph. With this caveat,
I hope a needless caveat, I should like briefly to examine, as
source of both hazard and triumph, the conventions of structure.

    As every reader of Restoration tragedy knows, the basic
cast of characters is simple. There is a hero in love with a

heroine and loved in return by her; there is at least one other
character in love with either the hero or the heroine but not
loved in return; there is some authority that prevents the happy
union of the two lovers. This pattern is capable of a large, but
limited, number of variations, most of which take direction
from the blocking force, that is, from the authority which prevents the lovers' fulfillment. In general, the blocking force
resides in either a king or a father, the representative symbols
of public and private authority. That authority, to heroes and
heroines distinguished for their *pietas,* commands an absolute
deference. Given this pattern, we can infer the nature of the
possible plots. The blocking forces must intervene either before
or after the play begins. If the latter, if at the beginning the
heroine is free to be loved by the hero, the (perhaps tempo-
rary) success of evil must pull the two apart: the result is one
of a range of plots structurally similar to that of "the conquering general soon disgraced." In this standard plot sequence,
the hero comes home triumphant from the wars, but falls
quickly into disfavor at home. *The Indian-Queen* and *The
Conquest of Granada* embody similar episodes—there is nothing
novel about the device—but the pathetic play takes disgrace
and exile seriously as no full-blown heroic play does. In the
pathetic play, moreover, these themes take up the whole space
of the play, whereas in Dryden they remain mere episodes.
As for the second range of possible plots, those in which the
blocking forces have intervened before the play begins, they
usually end unhappily and often turn on the threat of adultery.
Again, this theme comes up in most heroic plays, since intense
jealousy marked intense love, but usually occupies only an
episode or two. The pathetic play characteristically takes narrative segments from heroics, blows them up to great volume,
and tries to make their bulk significant in new affective terms.

One finds this kind of development of common plots if
one looks, for instance, at the half-dozen plays of the nineties
which dwell on the miseries of enforced marriage and parental

ambition. In *The Conquest of Granada*, Almahide marries Boabdelin; this has no significance other than as a means to forestall Almanzor, to let Almahide prove her spotless honor, and to provide opportunities for rant and jealousy. Boabdelin's tone is that of the comic cuckold in Dryden's comedies, the hen-pecked Old Emperor in *Aureng-Zebe*, and the disillusioned Adam in *The State of Innocence*. An alternative, and more serious, treatment of the enforced marriage in the heroic play appears in Pordage's *Herod and Mariamne* (1673) or Otway's *Don Carlos* (1676). In these, jealousy extends over five acts, but it is largely a jealousy of possession and personal *gloire* on the part of the offended husband. Near the turn of the century, however, playwrights had deepened the theme of enforced marriage both psychologically and morally, without, of course, excluding jealousy. We find tragedies such as Robert Gould's *The Rival Sisters* (1696), in which the two forced marriages (made or intended) lead to the death of five principals and the ineffectual attempt of a sixth to fall on his sword. Gould preserves the ambitious father only to let him deliver the concluding moral:

> And O! hereafter may all Parents see
> This Story, and Example take by me;
> That to each Child they may alike be kind;
> Nor rashly part what Heav'n and Love has joyn'd. (H4ʳ)

No one has known since Gould's death how serious or cynical he was in moralizing; what is important is that he wanted people to believe that he had legitimately concerned himself with natural and unnatural uses of authority, with those infrangible laws of nature that set a secure basis for moral decision. In Jane Wiseman's *Antiochus the Great* (1702), one finds a similar ethical interest. Antiochus' forced marriage to Berenice is the hinge between Berenice's reciprocated love for Ormades, and Antiochus' obligations toward his cast mistress Leodice. Along with the usual secret trysts and wrathful discoveries, Mrs. Wiseman's plot leaves her the possibility of considerable psychological and moral depth, in Antiochus' mixture of guilt and annoyance about Leodice, in his rationalizing his spite toward Berenice as compassion for Leodice when he decides to sleep with her once more, in his letting vanity masquerade as righteousness, and so forth. Feeling and duty mesh in various ways, limited rather by Mrs. Wiseman's talents than by the constraints of the subject matter. When the theme of enforced marriage reappears in Rowe's *The Fair Penitent*, one year later, the complexity that had been growing finds an artist intelligent enough to use it with great power.[1]

One discovers the same sort of change toward the moral and psychological in certain stock characters. For some reason, it does not take place in the characterization of the Hobbesian "statesman," who remained popular throughout the Restoration. Perhaps because his evil always represented an easily moralized entity, an abstract presentation, he rarely attains any degree of personal intricacy. In Bevil Higgons' Malespine, who "Must Conscience drown as Harlots Choak their Infants" (*The Generous Conquerour*, C_4^v; Act I), and thus dissolve every bond of nature, amity, and civilization, we have the voice of Crimalhaz pretty much unchanged. However, the stock character of the menacing king must have seemed less abstract, for it does develop. *Antiochus the Great* shows one mode of development toward psychological and moral depiction. Another mode of development comes closer to moral allegory than anything else. Cibber's eponymous Xerxes, for instance, stages masques glorifying lust.

With this new moral psychopathology, if I am not stretching a point too far in calling it that, comes a vividness of detail that most of the earlier Restoration plays had avoided. In

1. For a discussion of Rowe's balance of didactic and emotional reactions in *The Fair Penitent*, see Frank J. Kearful, "The Nature of Tragedy in Rowe's *The Fair Penitent*," *Papers in Language and Literature*, II (1966), 351–360.

Dryden's *Cleomenes*, for example, the slothful king Ptolemy is interested in "Whores and Catamites" (C2ʳ). The Emperor in Gildon's *The Roman Bride's Revenge* lies in "lazy Slumbers," "On beds of Roses with lewd Whores, and Boys" (B4; Act I). On one level, the playwrights must use such candor because they have already committed themselves to sensuous candor in the love plots; furthermore, perversities add to the immediate shocks on which serial drama likes to thrive. On another level, the playwrights are generalizing from techniques explored in *Venice Preserv'd,* where Otway equates the physically and politically unnatural. The joint rule of reason and nature thus keeps its force in prescribing the iconography of corruption, and in compelling the audience to secure itself by the proper norms. Meanwhile, the luxury of wanton courts supports the pastoral and what it stands for. In this way, the tendencies toward allegory and toward psychology, which might seem opposites, lead to the same ethic. If the conception of character becomes heterogeneous, pathetic tragedy masks inconsistency through its use of a homogeneous point of view related to the protagonist and to the structure of natural law.

Another stock character who develops, or at least appears in a range of variations, is the lustful villainess. She is, of course, a carry-over from the Elizabethan convention of the lustful queen, which had produced among others Tamora (*Titus Andronicus*), the Duchess in *The Revenger's Tragedy,* and the Queen in *Thierry and Theodoret;* her heroic descendents are the Empress of Morocco and Nourmahal. Just as the hero had sought glory and the heroine love in the heroic play, the statesman had sought advantage or revenge and the villainess the fulfillment of her lusts. This oversimplification is suggestive: whereas the heroine was a virgin or a faithful wife, the villainess usually had some taste of sexual experience, and therefore defied duty. Because she embodied passion, she provided most of the disconnected rant in the play. Most of this does not change with pathetic tragedy. There is, however, a growing tendency to treat the lustful woman psychologically, with understanding, as well as morally. (Like the statesman, she had always been treated morally.) Zara, in *The Mourning Bride,* is such a woman. The intensity of her passion, a hot passion set off against Almeria's equally intense but chaster feelings, becomes less a mere physical craving than an analogue to a heroine's love. This half-sympathetic, half-hostile treatment gives Zara a genuine complexity. When Almeria sees that the body she takes to be Ozmyn's is headless she merely exclaims in horror and faints; Zara, making the same error, rants like the traditional tragedy queen:

> Ha! prostrate! bloody! headless! O—start Eyes,
> Split Heart, burst ev'ry Vein, at this dire Object:
> At once dissolve and flow; meet Blood with Blood;
> Dash your encountering Streams, with mutual Violence,
> 'Till Surges roll, and foaming Billows rise,
> And curl their Crimson Heads, to kiss the Clouds!
>
> (I3ᵛ; Act V)

But she grows calm over the body, takes poison, and dies like a heroine: "Hover a Moment, yet, thou gentle Spirit, / Soul of my Love, and I will wait thy flight. / This, to our mutual Bliss when joyn'd above. [*Drinks*" (I4). The unhappy Oryala in Mountfort's *The Injur'd Lovers* (1688) is an even more sympathetic example of unrequited love; and she is no longer the significant blocking force in that play.

A second modification derives the energies of the lustful woman less from unscrupulous passion than from regal position. Here the "love" can be virginal, since its endocrine force is supplemented by the imperiousness of station. The Queens in Dennis' *Iphigenia* (1700) and Gildon's *Love's Victim* (1701) fall into this category. They are female versions of the semi-allegorical slothful king described above. As women, they are successors of Dryden's Lyndaraxa; but they do not represent, like Lyndaraxa, a scheming abuse of heroic love through a sinister coquetry. They represent egoism in a world of self-abnegation, an ethical offense against humans rather than an unfair trickiness within the game of heroics.

The development of the lustful villainess becomes interesting for another reason. We have here one of the few demonstrable results of the actors' theatre that grew in significance as the seventeenth century moved on; it may be important to discuss this matter in some detail now, when we have before us a specific instance of the companies' influence on dramatic form. Quite clearly, I think, the history of Restoration tragedy is dominated by Betterton, Hart, Mohun, Nokes, Sandford, Mrs. Barry, and Mrs. Bracegirdle far more than is that, say, of Renaissance tragedy by Alleyn, Burbage, Taylor, and Field. As back repertory was built up, offering great selectivity in choosing new plays and opportunities for comparison of actors in old ones, such an actors' theatre became more and more the state of affairs. New plays began increasingly to be written for strong points of star performers, and the actress, now sharing equal prominence with the men, helped restrict the variety of plays by furthering type-casting:

> [There] is a mass of evidence to show that most of the Restoration dramatists knew and associated (often intimately) with the players, tried in general to fit their plays to the capacities of an acting company, chose or helped choose the casts for their own plays, sometimes consulted with actors during the writing of a play, and wrote parts for actors and actresses who were popular, personally favored, or typed. Under such conditions, it was almost inevitable that the player should influence the playwright.[2]

As it happened, leading actors were type-cast far less than leading actresses. Type-casting of Mrs. Bracegirdle and Mrs. Barry in particular shaped the various tragedies in which the two prima donnas appeared together. To some extent, the

2. Wilson, *All the King's Ladies,* p. 97.

same thing had been true of earlier Restoration actresses. John Harold Wilson points out the pairing of Rebecca Marshall and Elizabeth Boutell, Mrs. Boutell playing the "romantic ingenue" and representing "goodness and chastity in opposition to Mrs. Marshall's pictures of evil and lechery."[3] Marshall and Boutell were the first Roxana and Statira, parts which will illustrate the types for which each was famous, and they were succeeded in those parts by Elizabeth Barry and Anne Bracegirdle respectively. During the reign of William III, Barry and Bracegirdle appeared together in *at least* twenty new tragedies. Mountfort, Settle, Rowe, Dryden, Smith, Dennis, Congreve, Gildon, Granville, Motteux, Mrs. Pix, Mrs. Manley—all enjoyed the support of this team of virtuoso actresses. The earliest of these tragedies was Mountfort's *The Injur'd Lovers* (1688), in which Mrs. Bracegirdle played the distressed heroine Antelina to Mrs. Barry's haughty unloved Oryala; here their two parts can already be seen discrete. Mrs. Barry, trained in the high rants of Lee, stamps and throws off violent couplets: "Thy *Antelina*, she shall be the Pile / On which I'l burn, and as I burn I'l smile. [*Exit*" (F; Act III). Mrs. Bracegirdle, younger, softer, more innocent, murmurs, "Where then, Oh! where shall *Antelinas* [sic] fly? / In what dark Mansion, cover her Disgrace? / A Ravish'd Virgin in a stranger World . . ." (G3; Act IV). By the time of Settle's *Distress'd Innocence* (1691), the roles have hardened. Mrs. Barry's Orundana, obsessed with the idea of revenge, proclaims the greatness of her soul, and threatens that she has "hoarded up those Shafts, those Bolts of Vengeance; / Shall strike him Headlong, plunging, sinking, drowning, / Below where Heav'n has even the Thought of punishing" (B2^r; Act I); while Mrs. Bracegirdle, the beloved heroine Cleomira, greets the hero Hormidas a few moments later with the recollection of "what my Tears have been; / . . . with what waiting Patience I have watched / The trick-

---

3. Wilson, *All the King's Ladies*, p. 97.

ling Sand of Time's slow Glass . . ." (B4ʳ; Act I). The pattern
continues through play after play: while Mrs. Bracegirdle
languishes and suffers, Mrs. Barry storms, stabs, poisons cordials
and sherbets, concocts intricate slanders, and dies fuming. So
successful did it become that the rival company at Drury Lane
had to flatter the two ladies by imitating them, for example in
Mrs. Pix's *Ibrahim* (1696), in which the sweet and virtuous
Morena (Mrs. Rogers) meets the persecution of the Emperor's
mistress Sheker Para (Mrs. Knight).

At first sight, the effects of this pattern of type-casting
appear profound, also stifling. The dramatists seem to be trapped
in a circle of built-in cliché. If Barry and Bracegirdle were to
act—and it must have been mildly risky to try to proceed without them—they had to have parts long enough to make their
presence worthwhile. Each undoubtedly wanted to be seen in
the sort of part she did best, if only from vanity; while the
playwright and theatre management knew that these ladies
could draw an almost automatic applause from the audience.
This meant money. It also meant being able to turn out plays
faster, on the grounds that the actresses could compensate for
sloppiness.[4] If any proof of these suppositions is needed, one
may point to the repetitiveness of the plays themselves. And
yet, given the facts of theatrical life, one might be struck by
their inadequacy as determinants. The type-casting turns out
to be versatile rather than stifling, as witness the spectrum of
heroine/lustful villainess parts that we discussed above.
Mutations of the typical Bracegirdle and Barry parts could
range from Vanbrugh's Belinda and Mrs. Brute in *The Pro-
vok'd Wife* or Congreve's Angelica and Mrs. Frail in *Love for*

---

4. As Abel Boyer wrote in 1702, "Formerly *Poets* made *Players,* but
nowadays 'tis generally the *Player* that makes the *Poet.* How many Plays
would have expired the very first Night of their appearing on the Stage, but
for *Betterton, Barry, Bracegirdle,* or *Wilks's* inimitable Performance."—*The
English Theophrastus,* ed. W. Earl Britton, Augustan Reprint Society publication, Series 1, No. 3 (1947), p. 18.

Love, to Granville's Briseis and Chruseis in *Heroick Love,* where the virginal Bracegirdle becomes a chilly coquette while the sensual Barry plays the part of a passionate but honorable mother. Hopkins' *Boadicea* and *Friendship Improv'd,* in fact, saw Barry as the passionate and honorable mother of Bracegirdle.

One is safe in supposing that the playwrights were responsible for whatever was hackneyed or fresh, not the theatres or actresses or audiences. Since the actresses were versatile, furthermore, and since actors were not type-cast in quite the same way, one is also safe in supposing that the division into Barry and Bracegirdle parts came about for aesthetic reasons, or reasons of ethos, rather than out of mechanical compulsion. Taken all together, the tragedies in which the two women were paired represent a continuum of female psychology as the Restoration saw it and codified it, and as Restoration tragedy explored it and milked it through a series of confrontations. From this point of view, the better plays are not so much repetitious as investigative. While Barry and Bracegirdle made the enterprise seem empirical, by the naturalness of their acting, the tragedians inquired into emotions that had become crucial to pathetic drama, its "feminized" heroes, and its attempt to weigh the claims of passion and duty. That the tragedians' reasons were affective and didactic as much as, or more than, cognitive, does not blemish the potential importance of what they were doing.

Along similar lines, we may look at another external influence on Restoration tragedy, the public demand for comic scenes and plots. As early as 1681, in the preface to *The Spanish Fryar,* Dryden had sanctioned joining serious with comic materials—always, of course, excepting rhymed plays—with his rationale coming from the audience: ". . . the feast," he wrote, "is too dull and solemn without the fiddles" (Ker, I, 249). Dryden's word and Otway's practice, along with the convenience of the rabble scene in political plays written after the Popish Plot, carried the day. Not everyone favored comic interpolations: Colonel Codrington's epilogue to Dennis' *Iphigenia* (1700), for instance, denounces the "little Whorish Arts" of Dennis' dramatic rivals, who deck the "Tragick Dame" "like a trivial merry Muse, / Or a rank Strumpet, strolling from the Stews"; these other playwrights, unlike the chaste Dennis, have no shame about making Melpomene

> . . . with the Comick Muse,
> Walk hand in hand, Grimace and Posture use,
> Debase her Majesty and Terror lose.

The indignation of Codrington, who was a gentleman, a scholar, and the owner of a £6000 library, was not shared by the less delicate playgoing public; and authors continued to keep the "rank Strumpet" strolling. Even if the public had not cared one way or the other about the comedy itself, authors would in all probability have made use of it, so that they could employ conventional plots and characters, and yet not leave their audiences with a heavy, warranted, feeling of continuous *déjà-vu*.

With the particularly obscure playwrights, the comedy and tragedy hang together like Siamese twins, each living its individual, hampered life. One of the plays that offends worst in this regard, amusingly enough, is Richard Norton's *Pausanias* (1696), a play described in Southerne's dedication to it as an "Experiment, upon the Model of the Antients, and according to the reformation of the *French* Stage." One would expect it to have a single instructive action, and by and large it does. Norton, however, may have worried about its success on the stage: something must have induced him to stitch on a completely irrelevant comic opening with a foppish courtier (who does not appear thereafter) and two equally irrelevant comic scenes about the prospective marriage of a young Spartan and an infantile hoyden named Mawkine. Most of Norton's fellows were less sloppy, if also more cynical and tasteless in counterbalancing tragic effects. I have already mentioned George Powell's cheap shocker, *The Fatal Discovery* (1698), in which a son, through a bed trick, unwittingly sleeps with his mother, remains out of the country for eighteen years without realizing what he had done, and returns to marry his sister/daughter. Mingled with this tale of double incest, a comic plot shows a battle of wits among a clever wife, her jealous husband, and her would-be lover; because of a pretended bed trick, the two men end up crawling about in the dark, disguised in frocks, trying to find one another. Here, the bed trick and the crawling in the dark both echo the tragic narrative, while the hero's name, Cornaro, suggests the motif of cuckolding in both plots. Powell seems to have had no sense that such superficial parallelism might destroy his tragic effect. He wanted to make money—as indeed his whole publishing career indicates—and knew that comic subplots were popular, especially if they were integrated with the rest of the action. Even mechanical unity like this, of course, is a blind nod to an artistic practice that does not depend on the public's simple taste for entertainment.

When we turn to a playwright of the second rank, like Southerne, we find a far brighter use of comedy. I am thinking specifically of *Oroonoko* (1696), in which the subplot about the husband-hunting of the Welldon sisters supports and helps unify the tragic action. While the genre of the novel had encouraged Mrs. Behn to use description of Surinam, its customs and natural beauties, so as to set up a frame within which the pure love of Oroonoko and Imoinda could be played, the stage denied such techniques to Southerne. Instead, he invented a level of everyday style and action, involving whites, by which one can appraise the black Oroonoko. Upon this level, he picks up from the tragic plot the themes of disguise, parentage, marriage, and trickery, and employs them, as Lee employs his rabble scenes, to achieve both grandeur and naturalness in his hero and heroine. He also employs them to make moral distinctions. For example, the Widow Lackitt (whose name implies both her avarice and her lust) appears as one who "has no Conscience in a Corner; a very *Jew* in a bargain, and would circumcise you to get more of you" (B4; Act I). She is fair game for a swindle, such as that which Charlot puts upon her. She is also a moral parallel to the Captain, who has cheated the trusting Oroonoko to enslave him, and the Governor, whose lust for Imoinda leads him to cheat Oroonoko once more. Comic animosity against the Widow amplifies one's detestation for the others, while the talionic morality of her being deceived helps establish a norm by which deceiving Oroonoko appears all the more horrendous. And the heathenism of some Christians ("a very *Jew* in a bargain") prepares one for the inversion in action and style whereby the black are white; and savages, civil; and the heathen, Christians in fact. Southerne's final touch is to make the subplot-figures spectators of the tragedy, as far as he can do so without debasing the tragic scene. He thus provides some choric perspective upon the isolation and grandeur of Oroonoko in his suffering.

Dryden's handling of the double plot of *Don Sebastian* (1689) made him Southerne's master, in every sense of the term. The preface to that tragedy says what I have been suggesting, that one cannot completely explain Restoration tragic structure by reference to audience and genre:

> I have observ'd, that the *English* will not bear a thorough Tragedy; but are pleas'd, that it shou'd be lightned with underparts of mirth. It had been easie for me to have given my Audience a better course of Comedy, I mean a more diverting, than that of *Antonio* and *Morayma*. But I dare appeal even to my Enemies, if I or any man cou'd have invented one, which had been more of a piece, and more depending, on the serious part of the design. For what cou'd be more uniform, than to draw from out of the members of a Captive Court, the Subject of a Comical

entertainment? To prepare this Episode, you see *Dorax* giving the Character of *Antonio,* in the beginning of the Play, upon his first sight of him at the Lottery; and to make the dependence, *Antonio* is ingag'd in the Fourth Act, for the deliverance of *Almeyda;* which is also prepar'd, by his being first made a Slave to the Captain of the Rabble.

Dryden, had he wanted to, could have continued boasting about his narrative management of the underplot, about the way in which he first develops Mustapha's greed and rancor toward the Mufti (which Antonio later dwells upon to save himself and Almeyda) in association with the dishonest slave sale of Antonio, so that the scene of escape repeats the same act of thievery and proceeds from the same motives developed in the scene of first captivity. Dryden could have boasted that it is Antonio's being made to cavort like a horse, to impress prospective buyers with his health and agility, that prepares one for his later sexual vigor in the Mufti's garden: the forced animality is shown quite plausibly in connection with slavery, so that when Antonio is indeed a slave, his pragmatism and lust seem acceptable. In both these instances, the subplot develops the same talionic morality as in *Oroonoko,* by which the serious action can be appraised. *Don Sebastian* manages this smoothly and naturally.

Aside from the formal deftness that Dryden shows, his subplot means more than that in *Oroonoko* because his play deals with questions of justice, reward, and will. These questions come up morally and quasi-philosophically, while in Southerne they remain unexamined assumptions behind an affecting spectacle. I think we can see Dryden's reasons for making the parallels between main plot and underplot rather specific and involving the two plots so much one with the other, in the sharper focus of his thematic interests. Methods like Southerne's had served him well in *Marriage A-la-Mode* (produced 1672) and *The Spanish Fryar* (produced 1680), but his more serious concerns and matured craftsmanship led him to go farther in *Don Sebastian* even at the expense of popular diversion. Whereas Charlot Welldon's disguise bears only a formal relation to the anonymity of Oroonoko and Imoinda, or to the hypocrisy of Captain and Governor, Dryden creates far-reaching ideological connections between his plots, and pulls together seemingly superficial parallels.

The tragic incest of Sebastian and Almeyda can perhaps be seen foreshadowed in Antonio's fruitless affair with the Mufti's wife and daughter, and later in Morayma's mistaking her father for her lover: the elements of a father's will, an alien court, and cuckoldry are common to both plots. In both plots we have characters taking turns in captivity—Antonio, Johayma, and the Mufti in the comedy—and plans to ravish women (Almeyda, and comically Johayma) and ravish power (translated in the comedy into money). In both plots, we find themes of loyalty, tyranny, reward, kindred, disguise for reasons of love-jealousy (Dorax', the Mufti's), and the metaphoric conversion of religion and love into power or money. Finally, both plots use similar metaphors, such as those of animality or of clay: Muley-Moloch calls Sebastian and Almeyda "the Workmanship of Heav'n, . . . the porcelain clay of human kind," which Sebastian changes to "mouldering Clay" (B_4^v, C_2^v; Act I). Antonio later revises the image to "Our Northern Beauties are meer dough to these [Arabs]; Insipid white Earth, meer Tobaccopipe-clay" (G^v; Act II). Obviously, the creation of man supplies the metaphor, as it supplies the context for metaphors of bestial men, and this in turn leads to the ideological connections between the plots.

The sensual garden of the Mohammedans was notorious as a merely carnal paradise.[5] For this reason the Mufti's version of

5. Dryden earlier had made allusions to this sensual paradise, as for example in his epilogue for Lee's *Constantine the Great* (1684):

> . . . Mahomet laid up for ever,
> Kind Black-ey'd Rogues, for every true Believer:

it serves as a comic heaven, presided over by a hypocritic holy man and filled at odd hours with lecherous ladies. The events that take place within it parallel the events of this world, represented in reality by the political plot and the tragic incest of Sebastian and Almeyda. In this way, Dryden presents and negates the pastoral world that is endemic in Restoration tragedy, and replaces it with the more severe and more metaphysical anchoritism of the final exile. No other imagery could better serve these ends than that of the creation and the ordering of nature, as natural relationships are adjusted on every level: the Christian and the pagan, the political and the personal, the sensual and the metaphysical. Thus Antonio's position as gardener, which is ironic *vis-à-vis* the riotous world of the Mufti, actually leads him to prune and mow, on his own level, the corruptions of domestic tyranny, demagogic law, and false religion, by which the Mufti lives in relationship to family, country, and God. The activities of Sebastian and the Christians lead to the same sort of restoration of order within the state. Because Dryden wants to concentrate on Sebastian's final metaphysical act of will, he does not force the parallelism, but lets the subplot carry the mundane readjustments; none the less, the fact of Sebastian's and Almeyda's taking over their respective earthly thrones even so briefly, makes the point symbolically. That Sebastian's kingship does reassert real order is suggested by his giving the final blessing for the marriage of Antonio and Morayma, a union that the Moorish garden of carnal fantasy can urge forward but never complete within a metaphysically meaningful Christian world. The echoes of the tragic plot, then, sound in the comic plot, and then fade before a higher and more significant reality.

And, which was more than mortal Man e're tasted,
One Pleasure that for threescore Twelve-months lasted; . . .

Still nearer in time to the composition of *Don Sebastian* come the lines in *The Hind and the Panther* (1687) which mention the "full fed *Musulman* [who] goes fat to heav'n" (First Part, ll. 376–379).

Dryden's technical achievement in sweeping us from the farcical scene between Morayma and her disguised father to the superb denouement of the tragedy makes the seemingly diverse plots all one. He makes the transition by way of the rabble scene, which no Restoration dramatist used to more point. At a time when a few playwrights may have been beginning to take the crowd seriously—Southerne's *The Fate of Capua,* for instance, uses them for straight exposition—Dryden, through Dorax, presented them as a "skum, / That still rise upmost when the Nation boyls: / . . . [A] mungrill work of Heaven" (O3; Act IV). He draws, of course, on the conventional portrayal, but makes it ideologically significant. Even the Whiggery that makes one "Rabble" assure his fellows that "I have seen for these hunder'd years, that Religion and Trade always go together" (N; Act IV), fits in with the mercenary piety that the Mufti practices, and that has a thematic interest in the play. The mob, in short, are the political embodiment of the life of this world in its meanest terms. They serve as an appropriate transition between the chaos of the Mufti's garden and the important political scenes, because they partake of both; Dryden can keep the comic tone going while events grow more serious, and then, as those events make the limitations of the rabble ever plainer, dismiss the rabble with contempt, his transition accomplished. Thematically, too, he has exploited their presence, with their insistence on flattery and wealth as the rewards of loyalty.

The same insistence marks Dorax, who scorns the mob most, and yet must see himself as most like them in blind egotism, symbolized by his political and religious defections to serve a Mohammedan usurper. His claims on Sebastian are undercut, and he is returned to reason and duty. The Dorax whom physical chaos—war and jarring poisons—could not kill, had committed moral suicide, suggested in his change of name; now, through that obedience to his king which no crowd could fathom, Dorax returns to reason, in time to keep Sebastian from murdering both himself and his soul. Dryden's final achievement through these comic scenes is one of dramatic logic. After we have seen the Mufti and the mob subdued by force, and Dorax by reason, we are ready to accept Sebastian's reordering of his nature in confronting primal sin through force (separation), reason, and divine faith. Our consciousness of hierarchy, in desires and in will, has been kept sharp through the comic analogies in the play, so that we are free to appreciate the structural majesty of the conclusion.[6]

Needless to say, I have left most of what occurs in *Don Sebastian* unexplored, but I have, I hope, indicated the dexterity with which a great author could use comedy and the double plot as the Restoration understood them. Other functions, such as pacing, contrast, giving the play scope, are harder to talk about. The reader of *Don Sebastian*, or, for that matter, of *Oroonoko* will have to see for himself the art with which these functions are fulfilled. In any event, the use of comedy plainly is no more a concession to low tastes in the Restoration than it is in the Renaissance. The only difference is, I should say, that the Restoration needed comedy more, because the tone of its serious plots tended to be less varied by lyricism or wit. The risk of diffusion would have turned out to have been worth taking for more tragedians, faced with the alternate risk of monotony and of having to manufacture sensational devices to relieve it. Many of these tragedians, unfortunately, decided to chance monotony, and marched off into wastes where posterity has refused, with good sense, to follow them.

The sensational devices that served the Restoration as dramatic adrenalin have become notorious. In our own century they have cropped up in spectacular films that dote on gory chariot races, virgins tossed to the lions, and technicolor battle

6. Bruce King emphasizes the inescapable drive, in plot and imagery, toward this conclusion; however, he treats the subplot almost entirely as discrete comic contrast. "*Don Sebastian*," Ch. X (pp. 165–185) in *Dryden's Major Plays* (New York, 1966).

carnage; historically irrelevant as such films (and their stage equivalents) are to Restoration tragedy, they promote cynicism about Grand Guignol. More recently, the "theatre of cruelty," following the principles of Artaud, has begun to insist on the legitimacy of horror and scatology to scorch the audience with the absurd savagery of life. Perhaps, from an ethos as irrelevant to the Restoration as that which results from watching films, the sensationalism of its tragedies will now undergo re-evaluation. This is undoubtedly all to the good, for serious playwrights in the seventeenth, as in the twentieth century, did try to force the tragic world into the experience of the theatregoer through shock tactics—perverse entertainment and invigorating a moribund plot were not the main concerns of Southerne or even Crowne, I suspect, whatever may have been the motives of Powell, Cibber, or Mrs. Pix.

The least offensive of sensational devices was the introduction of children, a logical extension of the hero's commitment to a wife.[7] As the archetypal innocents, children appear as early as *All for Love* and continued to appear, pathetically, throughout the Restoration and Queen Anne period: "a young Gentleman," wrote Mr. Spectator in 1711 (No. 44), "who is fully determined to break the most obdurate Hearts, has a Tragedy by him, where the first Person that appears on the Stage is an afflicted Widow in her Mourning-Weeds, with half a Dozen fatherless Children attending her, like those that usually hang about the Figure of Charity." In the Restoration, children implore their faithless fathers (Gildon's *Phaeton,* Jane Wiseman's *Antiochus the Great,* Motteux' *Beauty in Distress*); they mourn with their mourning mothers (Mrs. Pix's *Queen Catharine*); they occasion pathos by being kidnapped (Cibber's *Xerxes,* Southerne's *The Fate of Capua*) and starved (*Cleomenes*). Among all these, perhaps the only play in which a

7. Arthur Sherbo discusses the use of children for pathetic effects, in the chapter "Repetition and Prolongation," in *English Sentimental Drama* (East Lansing, Mich., 1957), pp. 32–71.

child really has any substantial influence upon the action is Mrs. Trotter's *The Fatal Friendship* (1698): Gramont's fear that his helpless infant son will starve, and then that he will be murdered by pirates, forces him from the paths of virtue into mercenary bigamy (although of course he does not consummate the second marriage). Throughout an extremely tearful pathetic tragedy he is tormented by the prospect of his son's starvation and pain, goaded out of honor by familial love as some of his predecessors and contemporaries were by romantic love.

The children, even without having anything to do with the action, are plausible in most of these tragedies; and, considered as visual metaphors rather than as people, are not gratuitous. I think one must see the plausibility and dramatic significance, too, of more horrific stage devices, appearing as visual metaphors. The "mangling" of prominent characters is such a device. In the most extreme examples, such as Selima's madness in Mrs. Manley's *The Royal Mischief*, gruesomeness is foremost: Selima, running mad on a plain to gather up the "smoaking Relicks" of her lover Osman (who has been shot out of a cannon) into a "Horrid Pile," is described as "Stretcht along, bestowing burning Kisses / And Embraces on every fatal piece" (G3^v; Act V). The audience was deprived of seeing this enacted on stage; Banks, in his *Cyrus the Great,* was more generous. Abradatas, in that play, has been torn apart by hooked chariots; his love, Panthea, has reconstructed him, "pick'd and cull'd" his "torn-off Member[s]" from "Amidst an hundred heaps of mangl'd Bodies." Thus the two of them appear on stage. Cyrus, unknowing, tries to put Abradatas' hand to his lips, only to find that it has disconcertingly come off the body (H3; Act V). Such horrors were of course not new on the English stage—there is a man flayed in Preston's *Cambyses*—but precisely because they have no moral purpose in the Restoration (as Preston's flaying does have), they are more prominent, closer to seeming ends in themselves.

There are few exceptions to the amorality of Restoration

sensationalism. One might argue that Zara's romantic suicide over, and cuddling with, the decapitated corpse of King Manuel, becomes a spectacle of precise poetic justice in *The Mourning Bride.* He and she both fulfill their blind passions in appropriately ironic ways. In general, however, the precedents for Restoration practice are not Elizabethan, but Senecan. I have suggested earlier that the end of Banks' *Cyrus* comes from the end of *Hippolytus,* where Theseus places the "disjecta . . . membra laceri corporis / In ordinem" (1256–57). Other tragedies display what Seneca only described; without the convention of the Senecan *nuntius* or the French *tirade,* the late Restoration stage had little choice but to display, if it was to make the horror plain to the audience. The comparisons with Seneca suggest, once more, that sensationalism can have a didactic purpose—teaching Stoicism in Seneca; love, pity, and fortitude in the Restoration—even if it is imprecise, symbolically, in regard to the moral development of the plot. Crowne's *Thyestes,* with banquet scene, and *Regulus,* with the hero's historical torments unexaggerated, might plead rather direct Senecan precedent; as might, by extension, various other tragedies, like *Oroonoko,* in which the noble Aboan appears after having been scourged with whips and rods.

One becomes more skeptical about the mangling of heroines, if only because the sexual interest of seeing wounded or recently raped women must have acted against the more respectable professions of the tragedies. By and large, though by no means entirely, the worst playwrights resorted most to assaults on their heroines. One exception is Mountfort, whose *Injur'd Lovers,* a good play, has the King appear with Antelina *"disordered,"* specifically with "torn Robes and hair" and "swoln Eyes" (F3, F4^v, G2; Act IV). But it is Mrs. Pix who has a scimitar drawn through the gripping hands of one heroine as a prelude to a rape (*Ibrahim*), or brings on another heroine *"led by her Woman: her Hair down, Distracted, Wounded in her Bosome, and Arms"* (*False Friend,* I; Act V). It is Nicholas

Brady whose *The Rape* has the scene draw to discover "Eurione *in an Arbour, gagg'd and bound to a Tree, her hair dishevel'd as newly Ravish'd*" (E; Act III). It is Robert Gould, one of whose plays (*Innocence Distress'd*) uses the double incest plot that I have already mentioned, who managed to have the thirteen-year-old Miss Cross brought out *"mad, stab'd in many places, held by Attendants"* (*Rival Sisters*, H3; Act V), with orders in the script to tear her wounds wider, and also, one suspects, to widen the rents in her clothes. And finally, it is George Powell (who plagiarized the double incest plot from Gould[8]) who featured slashed and bleeding ladies in *Alphonso, King of Naples* and *The Fatal Discovery; The Treacherous Brothers* only involves poisoning and impaling, but then, that play ends happily.

In all fairness, even to the Powells and Pixes, we should realize that these wounded heroines shock the modern reader much more than they would have shocked the Restoration audience, with its experience of pillories, floggings, and the Bloody Assizes. At Bridewell, women were publicly stripped and beaten.[9] Burning at the stake continued to be the punishment for a woman who murdered her husband—the eighteen-year-old Mary Channel, who poisoned the man she was forced to marry, was so burnt in 1703.[10] Besides their having grown accustomed to brutalities around them, the Restoration audience

8. Eugene Hulse Sloane discusses this problem in *Robert Gould, Seventeenth Century Satirist* (Philadelphia, 1940), pp. 105–111. Powell had plagiarized from other Restoration playwrights, notably Settle, and it is hard to believe that he did not do so here, once Gould's death or disinclination to make his tragedy public permitted the borrowing to go on freely. However, my calling Powell a plagiarist is assumption, not fact: the story, after all, dates back to the *Heptameron* of Marguerite de Navarre (the thirtieth nouvelle), and was in the public domain.

9. Ned Ward, in *The London Spy*, ed. Ralph Straus (London, 1924), talks about the lascivious spectators who came to these whippings to have their "Beastly Appetites" stirred up (Part VI, pp. 141–143).

10. See *The Complete Newgate Calendar* (London, 1926), II, ed. G. T. Crook, 148–152.

had long been used to sensational effects on the stage. Past experience, along with inattention and dim lights, must have conspired to make wounded heroines and "smoking Relicks" less egregious than they seem in print, and far less egregious than they seem when abstracted as I have done.

Before concluding this discussion of structure and technique, we might pause to consider the curious detachment of many Restoration tragedies from their denouements. Up to the end of the play, one can never tell whether things will work out well or disastrously. The most striking example may be *The Double Distress* (1701) of the ubiquitous Mrs. Pix. That play ends by informing the world that Heaven guards and rewards virtue, and Providence in fact loyally intervenes; but Mrs. Pix long delays the climactic revelation, that Cytheria, as the result of a masked wedding and a bed trick, has not slept with her brother Tygranes. Empathetic bosoms flutter; the forlorn trage-dienne throws off flurries of interjections; Heaven and Mrs. Pix smile in the background—at last, in ecstasy, Cytheria realizes that Cyraxes, not Tygranes, has "revell'd in . . . [her] Arms" and "rifl'd all . . . [her] Charms." Bevil Higgons' *The Gen-erous Conquerour*, of the next year, runs *The Double Dis-tress* a close second. In this play, just after incest is averted between King Almerick and the heroine Armida (after embraces and kisses), the hero Rodomond's death is announced, Almerick brings a cup of poison to his lips, and Armida drinks aconite, "Whose mortal Cold congeals the Blood, / And Freezes all the Springs of Life" (L3; Act V). Then, in quick succession, Rodomond turns out to have been spared by a disaffected villain, Almerick dashes the cup to earth and is saved by another disaffected villain from imminent poignarding, and Armida discovers that her "aconite" was really a harmless liquor substi-tuted by a devoted servant. Higgons and Mrs. Pix were obviously virtuosi at this sort of thing, but they differ from their betters more in degree of oafishness than in kind. Particularly in plays like those of the "conquering general soon disgraced," which begin with a quick peripeteia—Tygranes in Settle's *The Am-bitious Slave* (1694) arrives a hero on sig. C3, and is sent off to the headsman on sig. C4—endings are unpredictable. Because of the emphasis on serial technique, the tragedies often seem to be a series of stimuli and no more. Thus, for instance, deaths could be falsely reported, leaving the audience hanging between impending joy and impending tears with no clue from the tone of the play as to what was to come—*The Princess of Parma, Victorious Love,* and *Alphonso, King of Naples* all use this technique.

In one sense, the very arbitrariness of the whole enterprise keeps the audience unsettled and makes the individual plays, in their own way, effective. In another and more important sense, such mechanical endings destroyed any chance that nar-rative and theme could co-operate in any Restoration tragedy. Such co-operation demands a certain climate of expectation within which the playwright can create a meaningfully causal universe. It demands a broader understanding of "nature" than the tragedians can provide; there are crippling inconsistencies in a genre that cannot decide whether it is dealing with Providence or salvation, an essentially absurd or a potentially satisfying society. In these terms, we can see that the narrow-mindedness of Rymer's fabulism might have served better than the pragmatic breadth of Dryden and Addison, in giving Resto-ration tragedy a cognitive as well as an affective focus. But poetic justice, which would have had to have been universal in order to have been perceived as anything but arbitrary, re-mained a dead issue, disputed but irrelevant to the course of tragedy.[11]

11. Poetic justice has been much discussed by modern scholars, e.g., Lewis M. Magill, "Poetic Justice: The Dilemma of the Early Creators of Sentimental Tragedy," *Research Studies of the State College of Washington,* XXV (1957), 24–32; Richard H. Tyre, "Versions of Poetic Justice in the Early Eighteenth Century," *SP,* LIV (1957), 29–44; and Singh, *Theory of Drama,* pp. 64–92. The odd inconclusiveness of these studies comes from the fact that to the practicing playwright, poetic justice was never a real issue. The didactic

In the meantime, the best playwrights carefully used known plots, largely from history or the classics; or, like Otway in *Venice Preserv'd,* they combined history with very obvious thematic material to make clear their dramatic intent. *Don Sebastian,* for example, begins early to set up the conflict between human will and fortune, which leads any perceptive reader to the realization that *temporalia* eventually will be cast aside, even though they may be sweet. Thematically, the interplay of hubris (pride, tyranny) and genuine spiritual power make the Oedipal sin of incest appropriate, while the submission of Dorax to his king foreshadows the submission of Sebastian to his Lord. *The Mourning Bride,* which foregoes a known plot, early sets up determinant imagery, which I shall discuss in the next chapter; it also declares, in Ozmyn's prison scene, its dependence on Providence, and indicates, with Ozmyn's symbolic rising from the dead in Act II, its theme of rebirth. Even so, its characters at times appear "so many ping pong balls rebounding off that did not.

suddenly materializing walls of circumstance."[12] If Congreve can be charged with such a flaw, what can one say for his duller brethren? Here, perhaps, is the gravest defect in Restoration dramaturgy, a defect that should double our appreciation for those tragedies that transcended it and our regret for those

---

12. I am indebted to Miss Sharon Saros for the phrase.
and the two must be unified in theory for poetic justice to thrive.
and the metaphysical had different theoretical bases during the Restoration,

9

LANGUAGE

WITHOUT USING THE ANALOGY TO MAKE VALUE JUDGMENTS, one may perceive interesting parallels between the language of pathetic tragedy and that of Euripides. Quintilian, in the tenth book of his *Institutes,* compares the style of Euripides with that of Sophocles: "Everyone," he says, "must admit this, that Euripides is much more useful to those who are preparing for the bar. For his language (which is censured by those to whom Sophocles' dignity, loftiness, and sonorousness seem more sublime) comes much closer to oratory; he is rich with *sententiae,* in which he almost equals those handed down by the sages, and he can be compared with any famous lawyer in his skill at verbal attack or defense. He is admirable in raising all the passions, and easily supreme in exciting pity" (X.i.67–68). Directness, argumentative strength, moral generalization, and passionate appeal all characterize the style of pathetic tragedy at its best.

Ordinarily, I think, these characteristics would seem related only by their sharing in "simplicity." If we see them as complementary parts of a forensic style, certain further connections come to light. For one thing, we can see the four characteristics in similar epistemological terms. Each is a conscious means of demonstrating some truth, and each involves (as the argumentative heroic play does not) a continuing consciousness of an audience for that truth. We need not, at least in considering the intention of the tragedies, try to decide whether the chief influence on their style was the kind of simplification called for by the Royal Society, or the simpler and easier pulpit style of the Latitudinarians, or a growing concern for imitating natural passions. Each of these, especially the latter two, had its part. But each should be significant for us only insofar as the sort of statement to which it is germane, empirical or didactic or mimetic, interested playwrights who saw all three as rhetorical complements. Whatever outside standards may be invoked, pragmatic rhetoric is the measure of propriety, as one indeed would expect from a tragedy whose affective theory deifies rhetoric and its emotional consequences. The potential success of plays with such a stylistic basis can be indicated from the comparison with Euripides, as well as from the evidence of the best Restoration tragedies; the actual failure of the "forensic" play resides in the immense difficulty of writing persuasive language that will work for audiences other than the most immediate.

A second point that arises from considering the four oratorical characteristics is that the tragedy that they mark will have a set angle of focus. An "objective" play, in which each character lives his own life with its own autonomy and individuality, cannot be written. Settle, in *The Empress of Morocco,* could give more or less equal weight to Laula, Crimalhaz, and the four principal lovers, just as the Restoration comedians could depict numbers of striking characters, because the heroic play and Restoration comedy presuppose completely established norms of action and schemes of characterization. Most pathetic tragedies, however, have no more than one highlighted area—Pierre in relation to Jaffeir, Dorax in relation to Don Sebastian, the relationship between Ozmyn and Zara (*The Mourning Bride*) —within an unequally lighted picture. Within this area, language and complexity of feeling alike are at their finest. Moody Prior remarks of *Venice Preserv'd* that "the speeches of Pierre are, in fact, one of the interesting problems in this play. Nearly every time an arresting figure of speech or expression appears, it turns out to be spoken by Pierre."[1] The "problem"

---

1. Moody Prior, *The Language of Tragedy* (New York, 1947), p. 188.

can be solved, I think, by realizing that Otway maintained a spatial unity in his play, as he would in an oration, so that the relationships between the parts could be kept implicitly constant, implicitly balanced despite the inordinate attention that would naturally be paid to whatever happened to be going on at the moment. Such a spatial corrective to the effects of serial technique is surely desirable, and was quite possible in a drama which did not allow its characters to change their moral tempers and thereby the basis of values and language in their characterization.

In connection with the forensic style, more generally, the playwrights direct their diction. Linguistic virtuosity dies away, as do complex metaphors and the ossified metaphors ("flame" for "love," similes involving the cedar for "strength") popular in the heroic play. Metaphors that remain tend to place the action in the context of nature (animal, storm, astronomic, and marine imagery), of fortune (death, wounds, captivity, the rich merchant whose ships go down), or of religion (sin and lures to sin, angels and devils, Paradise). Although at times these images become clichés and lose their specific connotative force, they quite obviously relate to the most important thematic and ethical interests of the tragedies. Other images, like "rich mines" and "downy beds," usually occur when one of these three contexts suggests itself—the mines and the beds, for instance, apply specifically to conditions of fortune, while images of light may refer (according to the situation) to any of the three.

Pathetic tragedy replaces much metaphor with scene-painting. Like imagery about nature, fortune, and religion, scene-painting stays close to the thematic and narrative interests of the plays, developing most often as a projection of an ordered state by a character in the midst of disorder. At times it seems an act of masochism, as a heroine lingers on her probable distress. At times it produces a sort of disingenuous bravery, as in Mrs. Trotter's *The Fatal Friendship*:

Fel[icia]. Love will supply my Strength; and as I can,
I'll labour for our Food, or beg an Alms;
And we shall find some friendly Barn to shelter us
At night, whil'st we repose our weary limbs.
But cou'd you, my *Gramont,* endure your share?
And if the Product of our Toils falls short,
Take cheerfully the Scraps of Charity?
Sometimes perhaps your Sleep may be disturb'd
By a poor hungry Infant's Cries; cou'd you
With patience bear it? Cou'd you in such a state
Find any Joy in me? Wou'd you not leave me,
Leave me, and my poor Condition?—My Love,
Why this? The Tears are starting at your Eyes!   (G3^v; Act V)

Felicia's speech is by no means distinguished stuff, but it may
illustrate two points. The first is that the imagined scene turns
on the possibility of an ordered state. The sequence of thought
in this speech moves from confidence (the world provides jobs
and charity) and sheltered repose, to questioning (as the two
subjects of lines 2 and 4 are taken up in the next pair of
sentences, still within the imaginary ordered state), to disorder
both in the imagined state (Gramont's desertion) and in reality
(his tears). When the imagined state grows chaotic, it dis-
appears, and reality returns. Within the imagination, physical
and psychological orders have been counterpointed, and rudi-
mentarily explored. The second point is that the imagined scene
is primarily psychological and only secondarily pictorial. Felicia
does not dwell on one realized picture at length—if she were
to do so it would be for psychological purposes, to prolong the
ordered state in the midst of her real chaos.[2] Both these points,

2. The set speech here closely resembles the kind of expository speech that
we discussed earlier in connection with *Lucius Junius Brutus.* Lee's criterion
of unity is the audience's direct realization of a state ('Titus' reaction to
Teraminta's undefined anxiety), while Mrs. Trotter's is the audience's empathetic realization through the mind of Felicia, but both authors subordinate
visual evocation to thematic. As in the better plays, in which a potentially
discontinuous reality is controlled through a homogeneous point of view (see

order and psychology, lead one back to the pastoral, to which these imaginative stases can be linked.

The same tension between imagined order and real disorder comes up in other set descriptive pieces. For instance, Pierre's description of Belvidera's eviction (I. 232–267), although it describes disarray, does so to bring Jaffeir to formulate in his imagination an ordered state, an order to be achieved by spreading the disorder that Belvidera is enduring: ". . . burn, and Level *Venice* to thy Ruin." Pierre's intention, and the formal pattern that his speech imposes upon Jaffeir's distresses, create for him the illusion of increased assurance, by making Jaffeir resolute. Another set descriptive piece is Almeria's discourse on the temple (*The Mourning Bride*, C4, C4′; Act II); this is the speech that Dr. Johnson called "the finest poetical passage he had ever read; he recollected none in Shakespeare equal to it" (October 16, 1769). Almeria describes the temple as "rev'rend," "stedfast and immoveable, / Looking Tranquility," and by this very tranquillity "strik[ing] an Awe / And Terror on my aking Sight." Here the physical order of the scene becomes the occasion for disorder in the spirit; but as Almeria thinks on her present state, menaced by her father and her suitor, the formal order of pillars and vaults begins to promise a haven for her body and release for her soul. At the climax of the scene, Ozmyn appears from the tombs as though resurrected, giving the material temple its spiritual meaning, and thereby completing the imaginative movement that Almeria has begun. She at the same time faints, in a kind of simulacrum of the death which the temple had seemed to promise, and re-

---

Chapter 7), and serial technique controlled through spatial and thematic unity, so these speeches try to maintain rhetorical and thematic control over their vivid, sensuous, or lyrical pictorialism through the focus of the single speaker. It may be helpful to think of this habit of resolving disorder through focal concentration as "Late Baroque," since "point of view," "spatial unity," and "focus" all suggest the analogy with painting. One should use art historian's categories most gingerly, of course, since they tend to distract attention from specific works.

vives as though resurrected to true love. The transfiguration of
reality begun in the temple speech now meets the challenge of
reality, as Zara enters, and fades into disorder with the lies and
tyranny at the end of the act. Ozmyn closes this sequence when
he finds himself locked in a real prison, not the false prison of
the tomb:

> But now, and I was clos'd within the Tomb
> That holds my Father's Ashes; and but now,
> Where he was Pris'ner I am too imprison'd.
>
> (E2; Act III)

Otway's and Congreve's uses of the set scene grow more compli-
cated than Mrs. Trotter's, but the basis for all three is very
much the same.

One special class of set scene-painting is the sensual description, sometimes a recollection, sometimes an imaginative
hypothesis. Beljame quotes some of these speeches, objecting
that in the late seventeenth century "there was still an eager
welcome for sensuous scenes and daring descriptions. Congreve
did not stint such things in his *Mourning Bride*. Mrs. de la
Rivière Manley, who inherited the mantle of Mrs. Behn,
introduced into *The Royal Mischief* a love scene which her
model would not have disclaimed. Granville's *Heroick Love*
has passages which are amongst the most risky that anyone had
so far ventured to offer to the English stage."[3] About one of
the effusions that Beljame would have found distasteful,
Mountfort's Dorenalus (*The Injur'd Lovers*) protests:

> Oh! how you hung on the related Joyes
> You had possest the last dear happy night.
> With such delight you dwelt upon the Tale,
> You tasted 'em again in the description.   (E2; Act III)

3. Alexandre Beljame, *Men of Letters and the English Public in the
Eighteenth Century, 1660–1744* (London, 1948), p. 227.

The audience tasted 'em too, which partly explains Mountfort's and his contemporaries' use of such speeches; this sort of appeal, as I mentioned in Chapter V, began with Lee. But the speeches also have thematic functions, in casting a cruel reality (present or impending) against a backdrop of potential rapture, physical and emotional. The extent to which those in the audience taste the joys in the description marks the extent to which the potential rapture will strike forcibly into their experience, so that they can comprehend in immediate, empathetic terms the full meaning of the loss that they see on stage. Even salaciousness becomes a means of drawing sympathy; unintentionally the playwrights convert lust to morality. For this sort of developed emotional apprehension of reality, involved one way in the sensual description, a slightly different way in the imaginative scene, metaphors would not do, would not prove the point. The technique that the pathetic play substitutes for metaphor sacrifices grandeur and intellect for an intensity of realized feeling.

The lines that I have been quoting come from what one might call the "middle style" of Restoration tragedy. The verse in this style, as in the middle style of all Restoration verse, tends to be highly patterned, in the way, as we saw, that the opening speech of *Lucius Junius Brutus* is highly patterned. It carries the burden of thematic and narrative development in the play and is the most controlled and metaphorical of the three styles. Since its purpose is to imitate normal speech, its control and balance are verbal and syntactic, not prosodic. In *Lucius Junius Brutus,* the verse line maintains the importance that one would expect in the work of an ex-rhymester; if we look again at Felicia's speech from Mrs. Trotter, we will see less prosodic influence in its pattern; and a radical example, like the following broken stichomythy from Mountfort's *Injur'd Lovers,* obliterates all sense of verse lines, though not of an iambic rhythm, to render the terse dialogue. Rheusanes tells Ghinotto that Ghinotto's ambitious plans to marry his daughter Antelina to the King have resulted in Antelina's being raped:

Rhe. Who left his Daughter here?
Ghi. I did.
Rhe. On purpose?
Ghi. To meet the King.[4]
Rhe. To hear his Love.
Ghi. Ay, and receive it too.
Rhe. He has been here *Ghinotto.*
Ghi. I'm glad on't.
Rhe. He has made Love too.
Ghi. Better.
Rhe. High, mighty, pressing Love.
Ghi. More like a Prince.
Rhe. More like a Fiend of Hell.   (G2; Act IV)

And he draws the disarrayed Antelina in to confront her father. It is an effective scene, but the decorum is no longer, as it had been in the heroic play, the decorum of a poem. The fruit of the Dryden-Howard controversy, and Howard's eventual victory, appears unmistakably in this middle style.

The other two styles of Restoration tragedy are not really the high and the low, but the style of rant and the style of pathos. (I am excluding the comic scenes, of course.) Both are uncontrolled and free of metaphors, loose in syntax, and useless except as a supplement to past action or to a visual sequence of events. Since anyone who has read a reasonable amount of Restoration tragedy needs no illustration of rant, I shall provide none. The pathetic style is more interesting, since it is mimetic rather than conventional, and therefore can achieve precise effects instead of general tumidity. Here, one finds still further breaking down of verse structure, even of iambic rhythm. Pauses, once the prerogatives of actors, sprout in the text. Mrs. Trotter's Duke of Lorrain and his Marguerite must part (*The Unhappy Penitent*); they do so gaspingly:

Lor. [My heart] . . . softens, seems to shake my Resolution,
And I grow tame in gazing—Thou shalt not triumph—

4. The text of the play mistakenly reverses the order of this question and answer.

I disdain—my Soul resumes her self—
She shall not—   *Mar.* If e'er *Lorrain*—
   Lor. Do not talk—
I must not stay to hear thee—think not—never—
I will not see thee more— . . .   (G2; Act V)

Another version of the pathetic style approaches the style of
rant in its use of the exclamation and the middle style in its
patterning; it differs from both in that its exclamations are not
words but gasps, sighs, and shouts, and that its patterning consists in mere repetition. The master of this style is Charles
Gildon, beyond any question. In some 107 lines of his *Love's
Victim*, between Guinoenda's announcement of her poisoning
(G3ʳ) and Rhesus' fainting from grief (G4ʳ), Gildon manages
to work in no fewer than thirty-four "Oh's" and ten other
assorted interjections (for the curious: two "Alas's," seven
"Ah's," and a "Ha"). But no quantitative count can supplant
the shiver of seeing Gildon's style in context. We may look at a
rather long but entertaining passage from the third act of
Love's Victim, in which King Rhesus, who has been shipwrecked on the coast of Bayonne, meets his wife, Queen
Guinoenda, who has been shipwrecked at a different time on
the same coast. One should notice the subordination of speech
to theatrical events, the language's almost complete impregna-
bility to metaphor, and Gildon's extraordinary openhandedness
with exclamation marks:

   Guin[.] Ha! that Voice I'm sure's no Strangers. No—
And now I view thee well, I see my *Rhesus!*
O! *Rhesus! Rhesus!* for it must be thee!
   Rhes[.] Ah! well you know the sad Remains of *Rhesus!*
   Guin. Oh! late arriv'd to thy desiring Wife!
   Rhes. Thou art my *Guinoenda* then?
   Guin. 'Tis I indeed, it is your *Guinoenda!*
   Rhes. 'Tis she! 'Tis she! it is my *Guinoenda!*
O! my life! my Soul!
   Guin[.] O! my love! my All!

Rhes. Oh I have so much to say,
I know not how, or where I shall begin!
I have a thousand things to ask and tell!
   Guin. Beyond belief! almost beyond my Hopes,
I clasp my *Rhesus!*   [*Embrace.*
   Rhes. As I do thee, when I most fear'd I'd lost thee!
   Guin. See, see, thy little Off-spring too have caught
Our spreading Joy! see how they wait t'embrace you!
   Tyrel. My Father!
   Man. My dear; dear Father!
   Rhes. My Children!   [*they all embrace him.*
   Guin. My King!
   Rhes. My Queen! let me embrace you all!   [*Embraces them*
O! indulgent heav'n! O thrice happy Shipwreck! [*one after*
That cast me on my only hopes away!   [*another.*
                         (D2)

The tendency of accurate mimesis is towards prose. Lines of irregular length and irregular quantity, lines of sobs and cries, lines of "real" men and women—all these led to prose tragedy, as one by one the social, poetic, theoretical, and philosophic assumptions of tragic decorum began to wither. During the reign of William III two prose tragedies actually appeared. One, *The Czar of Muscovy* (1701), came from the pen of the inexhaustibly ingenious Mrs. Pix. She does nothing more than put a typical Restoration plot into prose rather than verse. Her writing in prose comes as no surprise to anyone who has read her poetry; ten lines from *The False Friend* (1699) will serve as an example:

   Adel[laida]. These are a Bridegroom's Extasies—
But, my *Brisac,* woo't thou talk
Thus, when, after many Rowling Years,
Thou has lost that Name; when I have lost
The mighty Charm of being new;
Nay, perhaps when both our Angry Fathers with Hatred
May pursue us; Drive us among humble
Villagers: Thou an Inhabitant of some Barren

> Plain; and I the Mistress only of a little Cell:
> Woo't thou then revive me with Love like this?   (C4; Act II)

There is not a regular line here, and only two which are even decasyllabic. From such a poetess one may well await the onset of prose. *The Czar of Muscovy* itself is not a distinguished piece of work, and in every respect other than its prose it is quite conservative, perhaps from fear that too much novelty might be unpalatable to the audience. Demetrius is the typical usurping tyrant who abandons the woman forced by her ambitious father to marry him. There are two pairs of lovers, pastoral appeals, a rebellion, an attempted rape, disguises, good and bad generals—in short, a wide selection of the expected trappings. One device in particular, that of having the heroine dragged along as she clutches her beloved (D^v; Act II), had been used by Mrs. Pix in both *The False Friend* and *Queen Catharine*: it is not too much to assume that she worried about the success of a play in prose, and tried to use tested stage effects as much as possible. She also tried to disguise the female authorship, so as not to provoke anti-feminist catcalls, and chose her theme to capitalize on the excitement of Peter the Great's recent visit to London. Her precautions seem to have made little difference to the play's success, literary or theatrical.

While *The Czar of Muscovy* eases into prose because the ideal of tragic decorum had grown so flabby, Durfey, in his two-part *Massaniello* (1700; 1699), the other prose tragedy of William's reign, understands and uses the principles of decorum with daring. He wrote with almost a quarter-century's experience as a prose comedian, and he knew very well how to manage low dialogue and situations. Thus he chose the story of the fisherman Massaniello who led a people's revolt against the Neapolitan regime, became King of Naples, and then was destroyed. Within this context, Durfey gives the devices of Restoration tragedy a plausible basis, the anarchic brutality of the mob. He presents the ingenue Fellicia with *"Her Hair dishevel'd, and Mouth Bloody, as Ravish'd"* (Part II, G2;

Act V). The beautiful Belleraiza, in the next scene, scarcely escapes from being publicly stripped naked. In return, the second part ends with *"the Trunk* of Massainello [sic] *Headless and Handless, dragg'd by Horses, his Head and Hands fastned to a Pole"* while his wife and two confederates hang gibbeted behind him; Part I has only offered, propped on poles, two villains' heads, from one of which Massaniello rips the beard. Pomp, apparitions, pastoral appeals, and tyrannic lust also link the technique of *Massaniello* with that of most of the tragedies that we have discussed; but here a new kind of verisimilitude is achieved.

What Durfey has done, and done handsomely for the most part, is to accommodate the serious and the comical without violating either social or dramatic decorum. Because the audience is not asked to view vulgar workmen and tradesmen sympathetically, Durfey can write a serious play about them, "serious" not in the sense of "sober" but of "large, comprehensive." He can give Massaniello a wife named Blowzabella and a secretary named Rock Brasile, give Blowzabella a maid named LaPoop and a valet named Dick Pimpwell, so that the rabble cannot strut above their proper stations except in an upside-down world. He can show their power, their vulgarity, their unreason, and their anarchy as matters of deadly importance. *Massaniello* is a Tory play written while Whiggery was in power, and thus it can claim kinship with the attitude of the greatest Augustan satire. Supported by its politicking and its anti-Jesuit scenes, it is an elongation and enlargement of the ordinary rabble scene into a satiric indictment of mob rule. While Massaniello remains a coarse but disinterested, just, and brave ruler, his reign is good; when he stoops from monarchy and allows his passions, represented by the ambitious Blowzabella and other relatives (i.e., the rabble), to govern him, Durfey damns him.

The overall treatment of language, the exploitation of prose, is brilliant. Here is Blowzabella, *"awkerdly dress'd and deck'd*

with Jewels" so as to look like a great lady; Don Tiberio, whom
she lusts after, has said that he desires something for the
Duchess:

> *Blowz.* Oh, gad so, the Dutchess my Prisoner; and you
> desire—why look, my Lord, if we should all have our
> Desires, what would the World come to? Why you may
> desire one thing, and I may desire another thing, when as
> things may happen, you can neither have your thing, nor I
> have my thing; oh my word, this is a great thing to consider
> of—and you must think I know my Post, my Lord[,] what
> I must do; great things now.   (Part I. D4; Act III)

The flustered, pompous stupidity of this speech, the coarseness
and intellectual poverty, and the realistic imitation of a garrulous
parvenu are quite masterful. In particular, the unconscious
double-entendres on "thing" and "post" characterize and illuminate as well as entertain. These people are funny, and, for
the same reason, menacing when their folly grows powerful.
Their proper decorum is the language of prose comedy that
Durfey gives them. The "high" characters are given a natural
but more elevated prose, which both differentiates them from
the rabble and keeps them within the same conventions of
verisimilitude. In other words, the prescriptions of decorum
and of accurate mimesis here coincide, as they had in much
Restoration comedy, and the precise social distinctions made
possible enabled Durfey to write a peculiarly social tragedy, a
play of frequent excellence and great originality.

No matter how good *Massaniello* might have been, it could
not have had a great following. In fact, it had none, and
probably little success, since it has remained so extremely
obscure. Its historical importance, like that of *The Czar of
Muscovy,* is as a symptom of the breakdown of decorum and
the drive toward accurate mimesis. Both plays, however, took
advantage of the theatre companies' zeal for novelties that
might blunt the effect of Collier's attacks. As the furor over
Collier subsided, Rowe and Addison turned the course of

tragedy into more conservative channels. The radicalism of *Massaniello* died, and the slow slither into prose that marks *The Czar of Muscovy* was halted. None the less, one should not underestimate the importance of the technical and sociological problems that the very existence of such plays posed. These problems lie at the heart of Restoration tragedy, in some ways at the heart of any poetics, and under one guise or another they continued to plague tragedy for the next two centuries.

Before leaving the subject of language, I should like to turn once again to imagery and metaphor. We have seen figurative language limited by epistemology and thematic concentration, replaced by set descriptions and sensuousness, and banned from rant and pathos. Finally, we have seen the movement toward prose slight these most highly "poetic" of poetic devices. Except for looking at the groups of metaphors that recur, however, we have not yet worked toward any positive understanding of their actual functions. Since I have touched upon the use of metaphors in Otway and in *Don Sebastian,* and others have talked about the language of *All for Love,*[5] we might examine the next best tragedy of our period, Congreve's *Mourning Bride,* to see what a capable poet and great writer of prose tried to do with figurative language. I need not say that Congreve's procedure was atypical in its intelligence: a hack's tragedy would show hack work in this respect as in any other, and while hack work often displays matters (like general characteristics of style) at their simplest, it is not likely to be of much use in exploring potentialities of organization. Congreve's tragedy is not eccentric, however, in that he does not go outside the bounds that his genre stakes out, and in this sense his excellence is very much that of his age and its tragic style.

5. Most notably, Prior, *The Language of Tragedy,* pp. 197–211; see also the connections made between style and theme in *All for Love* by R. J. Kaufmann in his thought-provoking but (I think) gravely uninformed article, "On the Poetics of Terminal Tragedy: Dryden's *All for Love,*" included in *Dryden: A Collection of Critical Essays,* ed. Bernard N. Schilling (Englewood Cliffs, N.J., 1963), pp. 86–94.

In discussing the temple speech in *The Mourning Bride,* we saw the way in which the sight of the building became a psychological and narrative source for the theme of rebirth. Congreve begins the play with images like those in the temple scene—images of the interpenetration of life and death, and of captivity. Woe has made the living Almeria "more senseless grown / Than Trees, or Flint" (B), unresponsive to harmony and nature. For her life means only numbness and agony, the outer and inner pains usually associated with death. The next act is actually to associate these two pains, narrowed to images of coldness and fear, with death in the vaulted temple, when Almeria briefly lapses from her posture as tragedy heroine. Here, at the beginning, she is fully a Mourning Bride, and sees nature as corrupt, both in the cruelty of her royal father and in the gluttony of the sea that has swallowed Alphonso; ascending from the natural, the familial, and the political, she accuses Providence:

> Why is it thus contriv'd? Why are all things laid
> By some unseen Hand, so, as of consequence
> They must to me bring Curses, Grief of Heart,
> The last Distress of Life, and sure Despair.   (B2)

Within this context, her tears are a parody of Alphonso's supposed death, as she drowns this world in grief: although she has been saved "floating on the Waves," her eyes will remain "swoll'n and watry," a "Torrent of . . . Grief," so that she is "drown'd / In Tears" while the "Damps of Grief" "scatter all / The dire collected Dews upon [her] poor Head" (B2ᵛ, B3).

Connected with these watery images are those of sinking and captivity, beginning with the burial of Anselmo, who had been "cruelly / . . . kept in Chains," the interring of Alphonso in the sea and in Almeria's heart, and the "double, double Weight of Woe" that King Manuel brings. Almeria's grief becomes an "unsuspected Hoard" and her fidelity, an "incumbent Debt." The only positive image in the opening of the play is that of light, the "bright Heav'n" which is Alphonso's kingdom, and which is the antithesis of Almeria's black. Fittingly, she thinks of Gonsalez' praise of his son as "gild[ing]," while Gonsalez ironically picks up the image as he enters to announce victory:

> Be ev'ry Day of your long Life like this.
> The Sun, bright Conquest, and your brighter Eyes,
> Have all conspir'd to blaze promiscuous Light,
> And bless this Day with most unequal Lustre.   (B3ᵛ)

Almeria then returns it: "My Lord, my Eyes ungratefully behold / The gilded Trophies of exterior Honours" (B4).

This imagery, all taken from the first 250 lines or so, is thematic. For that reason one would expect it to recur, and it does. The images of ocean are least interesting because they lose most of their narrative plausibility when Ozmyn/Alphonso appears alive. Shakespeare, whose metaphors are often iconographically allusive, might have continued using such an image; Congreve, whose metaphors are bound to the plot, cannot continue. He drops the moralization of the sea when the sea no longer makes a difference to his characters, although he does add weight to conventional metaphors by having moralized the sea in the first place: Zara, for instance, "has Passions which . . . tear her Virtues up, as Tempests root / The Sea" (F; Act III); or Gonsalez has "plung'd into this Sea of Sin; / Stemming the Tide, with one weak hand" (I2; Act V). Later, King Manuel, murdered through the course of providential nature, lies "welt'ring, drown'd in Blood"; Zara's rant over the corpse calls upon her heart to burst and "encounter" the "Streams" of the dead man's blood, " 'Till Surges roll and foaming Billows rise, / And curl their Crimson Heads, to kiss the Clouds!" The image comes to rest in Zara's poison bowl, which unifies the imagery of liquids with that of shared fate and that of gluttony, both of which were present when Almeria's tears imitated the "devouring Seas" in Act I, and both of which then took on independent life during the course of the play.

Zara's last words, "O now he's gone, and all is dark" (I4ᵛ), suggest the natural connection between the mingling of life and death and the imagery of light and dark. These two groups of images are joined at the beginning of the tragedy, partly, as I have said, through the striking visual effect of Almeria's costume of mourning, and partly through the traditional association of Heaven (death and eternal life) with brightness. In the temple scene, Congreve picks up the fatal sea image, reverses it by reversing life and death, and consummates it in light: Almeria's death, she says, will send her soul to a "refulgent World, where I shall swim / In liquid Light, and float on Seas of Bliss / To my *Alphonso's* Soul" (D; Act II). As Ozmyn/Alphonso appears from his father's tomb, imagination and reality readjust themselves and the imagery begins to dissolve. Almeria asks Leonora to hide her "from the Light," while Ozmyn modifies the earlier image of "gilt" in thinking her a "Form of painted Air" that sinks and falls, not swims. After the reunion, the scene ends with a reference to Heaven, whose messengers wear "shining Habits." Now Almeria's condemnation of the "unseen Hand" is echoed in Ozmyn's wondering at Providence "That thus with open Hand . . . scatters Good, / As in a Waste of Mercy." Almeria leaves as Ozmyn muses in atemporal imagination, "blinded" to the world (in this case, Zara) by the brightness of imagination and Providence, and therefore mingling life and death, "a Statue among Statues." In the next act Congreve brings up the same imagery when Ozmyn questions Providence in his prison soliloquy. The "Hand of Heav'n" leads him to a "dark Corner" of his cell, where he reads an atemporal message from his dead father, using the lamp in his hand and that in his mind:

>   . . . Reason, the Power
> To guess at Right and Wrong; the twinkling Lamp

Of wand'ring Life, that winks and wakes by turns,
Fooling the Follower, betwixt Shade and Shining. (E2ʳ)

When he resolves his doubts, he realizes that Heaven has indeed received his father's thoughts, "wafted thence, on Angels Wings, thro' Ways / Of Light to the bright Source of all." Through this sort of imagery, Congreve makes more significant the villains' mishaps in the dark at the end of the play; by counterpointing physical and spiritual lights, as in Ozmyn's musing on imagination, he can also invigorate cliché at the end, when Almeria "Gives a new Birth to [her] long-shaded Eyes, / [And] Then double[s] on the Day reflected Light" to find her husband at her side:

> Giv'n me again from Death! . . . can I believe
> My Sight, against my Sight? and shall I trust
> That Sense, which in one Instant shews him dead
> And living? Yes, I will; . . .

It would be tedious to harrow up all the further light and dark, life and death, and providential imagery in the play, or to expatiate on the analogies between the various sorts of physical and mental freedom or captivity brought about by Heaven, love, and kings. A more interesting procedure would be to examine one section of the play to observe the way in which images weave together. We may take, for instance, Ozmyn's prison interview with Almeria in Act III (F–F3), which begins with Ozmyn's fear that in embracing his wife he may hurt her with his irons or "stain [her] Bosom with the Rust." She cries out that he cannot embrace her, bound as he is with chains "which gnaw / And eat into thy Flesh, festring thy Limbs / With rancling Rust." Images of captivity, sharing, and wounds here join with that of gluttony ("gnaw / And eat") announced a few lines earlier in Almeria's assertion that they should

> Feed on each other's Heart, devour our Woes
> With mutual Appetite; and mingling in

One Cup, the common Stream of both our Eyes,
Drink bitter Draughts, with never-slacking Thirst.

With these metaphors established, the next movement of the
interview makes them spiritual, expressing a paradox: the
greater the joy of sharing, the greater the pain of isolation or
of inflicting shared pain on the loved one, while the refusal to
share "giv[es] me Pain, with too much Tenderness." Compared
to this mental torment, racks "are Beds of Down and Balm," an
image that is implicit in the fact of marriage and explicit in the
following discussion of the lovers' unconsummated marriage
and of Almeria's impending marriage to Garcia. Almeria, in
turn, recognizes that it is she who is tormenting Ozmyn by
their very love, and once more brings up, now in the spiritual
context, images of freedom and gluttony: "Am I the bosom
Snake, / That sucks thy warm Life-Blood, and gnaws thy
Heart? / O that thy Words had force to break those
Bonds, . . ." Grief takes over previously physical images of
wounds: it is "a Dagger," "Darts," a "Shaft." With this double
sense of the thematic metaphors now present, the conversation
goes on, reiterating the images in different forms: ". . . we
will feast, and smile on past Distress, / And hug, in scorn of it,
our mutual Ruine"; ". . . thy Words are Bolts of Ice, / . . .
shot into my Breast"; "[I will] bury me alive; where I will bite
the Ground / 'Till gorg'd with suffocating Earth."

It should be plain that the primary function of these images
within the scene is formal, that they give structure to the
interview just as repetitions and alliterations of words give
structure to an individual speech. The scene almost has the
structure of a gigantic aphorism. If space permitted me to quote
the entire interview, this point would be still more apparent.
Furthermore, the images clarify themes and bring them into
experience without extending them cognitively. Metaphors illustrate, but they rarely create truth within the rhetorical rules of a
forensic style. Their subordination to thematic interests thereby
becomes good sense, as does their restriction of range—indeed,

such restriction is the only thing that saves them from growing merely ornamental.

A third point to notice is their lack of moral meaning. In line with the whittling away of intellectual complexity in language, they have lost their iconographic significance. One may compare Congreve's generalized seas and rivers with those in *Antony and Cleopatra* to see how affective and perceptual interests have taken over from intellectual precision. Whatever depth of meaning the images in *The Mourning Bride* may develop comes only from the speakers or the persons addressed, so that metaphors have no independent validity as comments on those who speak them. At times they help set up moral contrasts between characters, but that is quite another matter. Their direct function is to be evocative, and evocative in terms of what the characters feel, not what is objectively true. No external reason exists for making physical/spiritual parallels between different kinds of wounds or appetite; the parallels are there because Ozmyn and Almeria feel they are there. Congreve may have put them there too, to dignify the mind by showing that its pains are worse than the body's. And at first sight, one might think that the assertion of Providence over blind chance, and of the spirit over the body, are analogous. Rhetorically and formally, they are; but intellectually one can hardly claim that an assertion of order and control is similar to an assertion of quantitative difference between a pair of independent sensations, mental pain and physical pain. The analogue is specious, part of a general procedure of loose praise rather than a serious and exact exploration of relationships.

Congreve uses other metaphors, of course, besides those we have discussed; none the less, from what we have discussed, one can see his method of operation. He deals carefully and intricately with those artistic problems that are central to the kind of tragedy he is writing. His results are quite legitimate, and quite different from the procedure and results of the Elizabethans. In his restraint of metaphor, his rhetorical pacing of scenes, and his subordination of the ordonnance of verse to that of natural speech, Congreve is very much of his time. I do not want to invoke the Arnoldian specter of "prose and reason," for there is much poetry and imagination in *The Mourning Bride;* but both move in an alliance with prose and reason, take certain norms from prose and reason, to a far greater extent than do the poetry and imagination of Arnold's Romantic (or Romanticized) ideals, and in a different way from the poetry and imagination of the historical Shakespeare, of Milton, or of Pope.

CONCLUSION

RESTORATION TRAGEDY NEEDS NO SPECIAL PLEADING. ONE should not pretend that most of it was good; most of it was poor. Most of the plays written during any period are poor, for the primary limitation comes from lack of talent. Many critics have charged that the very *Zeitgeist* of the Restoration starved compassion, generosity, and the tragic sense of life, so that its tragedy was too severely rational or too flabbily emotional, too frigid or too gushing, too regimented and neo-classical or too extravagant and unruly—only the plays themselves, regarded with the preliminary historical sympathy that all literature of the past demands, can answer such charges. This study has tried to provide the scholar and the critic with the historical means of scrubbing away the cant and impressionism that have crusted our subject. In fact, as we have seen, the tragedies are complex instruments to develop compassion and generosity; and, if I understand what "tragic sense of life" means, I should think that nothing is more integral to Restoration tragedy, in which the pleasures of the world typically burn with a desperate ecstasy because they are so mutable. Many of the playwrights abuse these legitimate ends, so that the question of sincerity always arises. Such matters eventually belong, of course, to personal judgment. None the less, the kind of aesthetic and thematic intricacy that men like Otway, Dryden, and Congreve develop in their tragedies, should guarantee their seriousness. Their critical consciousness becomes still another index of their seriousness.

Their drama was in many ways paradoxical. The new tragic theory seemed to strengthen generic criticism by adding a specific emotional province to each genre along with its province of style, and yet these emotional criteria were to destroy the idea of genre as men had known it. Critics claimed to follow Aristotle; but if one considers the definition of tragedy given in 1647 by the greatest of seventeenth-century Aristotelians, Gerardus Vossius, he will see the Restoration dramatists as strange partisans. Vossius wrote that *"Tragoedia est* poema dramaticum, illustrem fortunam, sed infelicem, gravi & severa oratione imitans. *Quibus & finem hunc, si voles, adde;* ad affectus ciendos, animumque ab iis purgandum."[1] Fifty years later, tragedy remained a dramatic poem, but the fortune in it had to be neither illustrious nor unhappy, and serious weighty speech had given way to a flow of natural rhetoric. Emotional effects, about which Vossius is so cavalier with his *"si voles,"* now dominated tragedy. And purgation was left in doubt.

Perhaps the greatest paradox of Restoration tragedy is its seeming austerity of rhetoric, its cramping of the metaphor, when in fact its mimetic technique makes the play itself a willing metaphor of the world. We have the apotheosis of a rhetoric of things—acts, feelings, situations—rather than words, as those parts of drama that had hitherto had a subsidiary and expressive effect suddenly became central. In its insistence on touching the heart, Restoration tragedy committed itself to natural mimesis, to an honesty of representation. Even the demand for poetic justice, which appears on the surface to foster dishonest manipulation, in fact reflected a commitment to "nature," a metaphysically informed "nature" which tragedy should map out. Supernatural and natural alike should be projected into the mundane terms of the stage. And if poetic justice sprang from a fidelity to nature, the procedure of playwrights who rejected it, and thereby rejected such transformations of metaphysics, surely sprang from a concentration on nature. Assiduously, these playwrights brought to maturity a

---

1. Gerardus Joannes Vossius, *De Artis Poeticae Natura, ac Constitutione Liber* (Amsterdam, 1647), II.xi.2, sig. f2ᵛ.

group of new formal elements—pastoral and its analogues—
that took the place of poetic justice and yet remained within
the bounds of the observably natural.

The paradoxes about which I have been talking were no more
than half-intended by the Restoration, as it used its newly
developing sense of history to place itself in the course of
human culture. Aristotle and generic criticism were part of its
intellectual past, rhetoric part of its practical English past; and
with both the playwrights came to their own accommodation.
This accommodation was neither a simplification nor a limiting
act of rationalizing. It was not a simplification because the
number of formal problems for the playwrights remained
roughly the same. Throughout this study, I have been trying
to show that the changes in perspective that we have discussed
lead not to elimination but to redistribution: each style re-
phrases, as it were, the idiom of its predecessor. Restoration
tragic theory grows this way, as do the structures of the late
heroic play and of pathetic tragedy. Accommodation with the
past was not a limiting act of rationalizing because if anything
dramatic flexibility increased. For proof, we have only to look
at the bewilderingly rapid changes in emphasis from Boyle to
Dryden to Lee to Otway, and then more sluggishly to Rowe.
Theatrical conditions, as I have indicated, kept the various
stages of this development from attaining the kind of polish
and force that they might: one has only to see that Harbage
and Schoenbaum's *The Annals of English Drama* has to devote
seventy pages to the four decades before Cromwell and only
fifty to the four after 1660, to realize that playwrights were not
being nurtured as they earlier had been. The limitations, then,
did not come from too much rationalizing but from too few
customers. As it is, the better plays show a fine artistic
conscience in converting merely affective requirements into a
complex aesthetic idiom. Pathetic feeling, heroic romance, hard
didacticism, and the standards of earlier plays merge into a
synthesis that at its best brought forth superb tragedy, like

Venice Preserv'd and *Don Sebastian*, and at its second best, narrower but accomplished plays, like *The Orphan, All for Love* and *Cleomenes, The Mourning Bride*, and perhaps the finer works of Banks and Lee.

None the less, it would be unfair to deny that Restoration tragedy has worn badly. And even if one would have to say the same thing about all but a half-dozen Renaissance tragedies, Shakespeare's excepted, bad wearing ought to be instructive. The answer is not, I believe, that the plays are "unnatural" and "melodramatic." A reader of Restoration tragedy who knows the libretto of *Aïda*, say, is amused by the long life of the Restoration clichés: the conquering general soon disgraced, the Bracegirdle and Barry female leads, the royal oath—even Radamès' last words to Amneris, "L'ira umana più non temo, / Temo sol la tua pietà" echo lines from Restoration tragedies. Nearer our own time, we can look at a film like *Gone with the Wind*, in which we have the death of a child and of a pure heroine, madness, physical anguish, violent spectacle, modifications of the Barry and Bracegirdle types, serial construction, and even an ending posed against the radiant sky of The Pastoral Ideal. The opera is still magnificently effective; the film, effective enough to give pleasure. The lesson that one learns, I think, is that a work of art that depends on the creative emotions of the audience as Restoration tragedy did, and as *Gone with the Wind* does, grows dated. Even the great Ibsen, braced and rouged by colloquial translation, has begun to grow dated in the mid-1960's. *Aïda*, on the other hand, shares with the finest tragedies of the Renaissance a fixed idiom: the formal complexity of its music and their poetry has an independent life, and continues to evoke a complex response. Restoration tragedy tends to subordinate formal elements. Contemporaneity made it affecting, and now entombs it from all but the scholar with historical imagination. This does not mean that its mode was less valid—tragedy can legitimately aspire to prose—but rather that the mode must keep renewing its idiom, finding continuing validity not in enduring artifice but in a stream of new plays and new audiences to fulfill them.

INDEX

Abrams, Meyer H., viii*n*
Adam, Antoine: on Quinault, 45*n*
Addison, Joseph: his aesthetics and Locke's, 22*n*; *Cato*, 121; on children in tragedy, 153; critical pragmatism, 158; on laughter of approbation, 100*n*; on Otway, 21; on pity and terror, 22; on poetic justice, 22*n*; mentioned, 93*n*, 131, 172
"Advice to Apollo": attack on Dryden, 31*n*
Allegory, in Renaissance and Restoration, 65–66
Alleyn, Edward, 141
Andronicus: A Tragedy, 68
Aristotle: and affective tragedy, 4, 13–18; his a priori criticism, ix; magnanimity and pathetic tragedy, 121; *Poetics* in England, 5, 9–10; Rapin on the *Poetics*, 10–12; mentioned, 182, 183
Arnold, Matthew, 180
Arrowsmith, Joseph: opposition to rhyme (in *The Reformation*), 31*n*
Artaud, Antoine, 153
Aulus Gellius, 116
Avery, Emmett L., 25, 43*n*, 51*n*

Banks, John: *Cyrus the Great*, 97*n*, 116, 154–55; *Destruction of Troy*, 96, 97 and *n*; diction of, 98–99; *Innocent Usurper*, 124; *Island Queens*, 96, 97*n*, 124; *Rival Kings*, 79, 88, 97*n*; *Unhappy Favourite*, 96; *Vertue Betray'd*, 96, 98, 99; mentioned, 90–91, 100, 102, 105, 110, 115, 134, 184

Barry, Elizabeth, 25–26, 141–44, 184
Behn, Aphra: *Oroonoko*, 146; on popularity of heroic play (in *The Emperor of the Moon*), 26–27; mentioned, 121, 165
Beljame, Alexandre: on indecency of Restoration tragedy, 165
Belon, Peter: opposition to rant (in *The Mock-Duellist*), 39*n*
Bentley, G. E., 128*n*
Berkeley, David S., 39*n*, 98*n*
Betterton, Thomas: nominal author of *History of the English Stage*, 26*n*; his rant, 32–33; mentioned, 130, 141, 143*n*
Blackfriars Theatre, 128
Boas, Frederick S.: on Edward Howard's *The Usurper*, 72
Boccaccio, Giovanni, 4
Booth, Barton, 25*n*
Bond, Donald, 32*n*
Borgman, Albert S., 26*n*
Bossuet, Jacques-Bénigne: on catharsis, 13*n*–14*n*
Boutell, Elizabeth, 142
Bowers, Fredson: on Falkland's *The Mariage Night*, 65*n*
Boyer, Abel: on Restoration actors, 143*n*
Boyle, Roger, Earl of Orrery: freedom from rant, 38; *The Generall*, 66; generic decorum, 70–71; *Tragedy of Mustapha*, 25, 56, 84; *Tryphon*, 25*n*, 132; mentioned, 56*n*, 100, 183
Bracegirdle, Anne, 141–44, 184
Brady, Nicholas: *The Rape*, 155–56
Branam, George, 26*n*

186